*If a man does not keep pace with his companions,*
*perhaps it is because he hears a different drummer.*
*Let him step to the music which he hears,*
*however measured or far away.*

Henry David Thoreau
from *Walden*

## *Editor's Note*

This book has been a trans-Atlantic venture, involving the sharing of ideas and experiences across miles and over some time. Paddy Clarke's daughter Samantha celebrates her 21st birthday on the eve of the publication of *To A Different Drumbeat*. She was born and raised in Great Britain. Holly Kofsky's Naomi and Benjamin are growing up in California on the West Coast of the United States. Jenni Lauruol's Marie, Patrick, and Daniel were born in France and now know England as their home. Jenni is herself American and her husband French. We've been greatly assisted by Helen Allen, Lyndsey Gill, Susannah Burnett, Catherine Gellhorn, Mandy Fincham and Doug Sim, also from England. The Artist, Tom Nelson, lives and works in Kansas City, Missouri, U.S.A.

We have sought to retain a simplicity and sincerity in thought and style, and hope to reach other parents and friends who are faced with the uncertainties and questions posed by a child with special needs. If by sharing experiences and insights we can make their roles a little less lonely, a bit more positive, then we will have achieved our aim.

Children with handicaps can show all of us – and society in general – new horizons, qualities, potential and inner depths we've never imagined. To these children everywhere, and to their carers, we dedicate this book.

Judith Large
Gloucestershire, England

# Contents

# *Foreword*

When I first read this book one thing shone through like a beacon. This is a book *about* relationships and it is a book *for* parents. It might seem at first glance it is only about the relationship of a parent and a special child and only for parents with special children. Indeed the essence of this book has come from that very source and will have very particular meanings to parents and families of special children. However, the thoughts, feelings and experiences which shape and fill this book have something important to say about *all* relationships, is of direct relevance to every parent and should be read by all professionals who seek to work with and support these exceptional children, their families and friends.

It is a book which gives a number of honest and direct pictures. It follows the experiences of several parents from the early babyhood of their children to, in one case, a coming of age at 21. These parents, who were challenged into courage by circumstances, have many things in common and these common threads for me lead to a theme. It is a theme of whole-hearted love. There are no half-hearted relationships here. Their stories are not necessarily easy ones, nor are they romantically rosy, they are real, and this reality can be difficult. Nevertheless it is often joyful and surprising.

One strong message here is a message about choice. We always have a choice, even with a seemingly immovable fact. We can choose to change our relationship to that fact. We can choose to change from closed anger or deep sadness or even resentfulness to openness, calmness and inner peace. We can choose which things to get angry about and which things to accept. In this choosing we change the whole picture. For changing the nature of our relationship creates a kaleidoscope effect. One small shift and a very different pattern appears. In this book there are practical suggestions on everything from play to incontinence, music to guilt, but above all there are real experiences. The parents of Samantha, Naomi, Benjamin, Marie, Daniel, Keziah, Katy and Catherine have told their stories in a strongly focused and personal way.

When I was asked to write a foreword to this book I immediately agreed as I so very much could see the need for such a book. However, as I read the book I began to doubt my own fitness to write the foreword. Although I am a parent of two sons, Eric and Andrew, who are both "special" to me, I had not in any measure experienced the difficulties that parents of children with special needs live with on a daily basis. Then in reading the book I had a vivid recollection of an event which in a very small way reminded me just how special our children are. Therefore in common with the spirit of writing in a personal way, like all other parent authors in this book, I would like to share it with you.

In the early 1960's my sister and I were both young expectant mothers, she living in Manchester, I living in Turkey, where my husband had a two year work contract. My son Eric was born on March 14th, her son Paul on May 14th. We kept very much in touch through letters, sharing this new experience together across the miles. I was living quite primitively in a Turkish village with few conveniences and very little in the way of family support. Following an earthquake and a military incident I began to worry what might happen to my baby, if, for some reason, I had a fatal accident. I sentimentally pictured my family in Britain searching Turkey for my baby son. I then realised that beyond a first photograph they had no information to help them to identify him. It took some thinking about, however I finally found a way of casually inserting a detailed description of my baby into a letter home. "He is 22″ long" I said, "and weighs 11lbs 3oz. His hair is sparse and spiky and a reddish brown colour. He has a small "coffee" stain birthmark behind his left knee and another one on the left side of his lower back. When he cries there is a small "strawberry" mark between his eyebrows, which can become raised if he cries hard or for a long time." It was some time before I had a reply from my sister. She said "What a very interesting baby he sounds to be with all those flaws, my baby, of course, is perfect!"

I was stunned, my baby was perfect too. He was perfectly himself and I really had never considered that others might view him a in a very different way.

All of us who have children or who work with children will know that it is the very differences between children which make them special. So it is with this book. *To A Different Drumbeat* will be a special addition to every bookshelf.

Rennie Fritchie

# 1

## Imagine

*The following is an attempt to convey what it is like to be Laurie, a three-year-old, multiply-handicapped, visually-handicapped little boy with some measure of intelligence.*

Outside me is a muddle, and inside me is a bit of a muddle too. But inside is me and I know what that is. I can start from there...

I can feel the floor beneath me. I know the carpet, the hard floor in the kitchen, the rush mat in the hall and the grass, but that's funny and that's outside. I like outside. I like rain on my face and I love the wind. It moves with my hair and I laugh and when there's lots of it it takes away my breath. I adore the wind, even when it's only pretend with Mummy blowing in my face. I don't like the sun when it's hot but I like sand and I love water.

There are toys near me. I can feel them if they are put into my hand, I hold them tight and wave them about, but it's hard to find them for myself. Sometimes they are right by me, I just know they are there, and Daddy says "Come on, Laurie! It's still there, you can find it!" but my arm won't go there. Sometimes I can see a bit of it right by my eye, then it's easier to feel it with my mouth because my hand seems so far away and it's so slow. My mouth knows lots of things, holds them and tastes them and licks them and bites them. My mouth eats and drinks and makes lovely noises.

I know my cup, I know the shape of it close to my face. I like shiny baubles and little coloured lights and the crystal in my window, but mostly I like things that make a noise. I like little bells, rattles, people chatting, birds singing and music, lots of mouth sounds and rude noises and the newspaper crackling and the train in the distance. I like the noise of the broom but not the hoover, that frightens me; the water running but not the washing-up; I jump and sometimes cry when the saucepans clatter. I hate doors banging, a dog barking and sudden shouts because I don't get a warning, they just crash into me and batter me and I don't know they are coming.

I like to know what is going to happen, that tea is ready and Daddy has come home and then it's bath time and warm milk and cuddles, always the same. I know my own bed and my own buggy, my little brother (I don't mind surprises from him so much), I know our car and school and Grandma's house and ice-cream now that I know that it is very cold and funny in my mouth.

My mouth is very important. Mouths are for eating and drinking and blowing bubbles and kissing and talking. My Mummy and Daddy talk a lot, talk all the time, and I talk back, but it doesn't sound like them. I try very hard but it doesn't come out quite right...

# 2

## *Our Personal Journeys*

PADDY:

I look through the window and see Samantha in the autumn sunlight helping Father in the garden. Perhaps she would prefer to sit running stones through her fingers in her form of meditation or leisure but has been persuaded to carry branches to the bonfire site. They talk together earnestly – her short choppy sentences quite clear, "This big one, Daddy", and now she rocks with delighted laughter as Father stubs his toe and hops about. Then bubbling merriment engulfs her as the groans continue and she plonks down on the ground, doubled up with mirth. Father is joyfully caught up in the laughter, too.

This is the child considered at three years old to be so hopelessly retarded that the only course was "to put her away and forget about her for she will never walk or talk or recognise you." Even before this she was diagnosed profoundly deaf and visually impaired. At three years four months she was labelled autistic – "for which there is no treatment though you can bring her back in a year if you wish." At eight she stopped growing though she continued to spread widthwise and she could make herself understood by putting words together in her inimitable manner. She could walk though was not keen to do so but moved at the speed of light to the furthest ends of the garden when it was bath time or was being chased to recapture a vital book she had sneaked from Mother's desk. At fifteen an astute and loving teacher suggested (from previous experience) a new facet on her disabilities and Prader–Willi syndrome was eventually confirmed. Sam has a badly deformed spine, is often incontinent and hyper-active, sleeps fitfully and has a most powerful and loveable personality. A deeply cherished girl who radiates love and enriches the lives of most who know her.

To be the parents of a 'special child' confers a treasure house of experiences – a few involving sadness, tears and heartache occasionally dipping to despair but most about the power and joy of giving and receiving love unlimited; of trying and trying and succeeding, in the lengthy build up of minor triumphs into major gains and in sharing in a child's life which, in not running the 'normal' path is even more exciting, adventurous, merry and worthwhile than many who do.

Ever so often the question comes up "If you had known then what you know now, what would you have done?" The answer has always been that I wouldn't have missed it for anything. My twenty years journey with Sam has touched heights and depths and is a collage of countless decisions, often apparently having no connection with past decisions and not necessarily affecting the future, of learning to generate the courage and faith to do for Sam what seemed right to me, to enjoy and defend (along with her Father) the right as a deeply loving and committed Mother to work along the lines I chose and to relish Sam's successes and comfort her setbacks because that's what love is about. To have a handicapped child is to know all aspects of enduring love.

What I would have liked to 'have known' then were practical matters which would have allowed shortcuts in Sam's 'education', to have understood earlier that established teaching ideas are often not suitable for the handicapped and to avoid the mass of dogma and convention surrounding the upbringing of the handicapped. One achieves most by taking courage in hands and 'trying it'. Sam leaves formal education soon moving to yet more unknown paths. Her gift and mine to those coming behind is not to chart our story (that is for elsewhere) but to share our learning experiences and pass on what we know now.

*As I look back I remember*
*That when she was born I knew deep in my soul that our daughter*
*was a special child.*

*I did not know then that 'special' was a euphemism for the old term 'retarded'.*

*Special to me meant a gift beyond other riches.*
*I knew too, she would alter our lives for we loved children and planned a large family.*

*I was not able to have other children*
*It was meant we concentrated on this very special one.*

*And she has been a gift beyond other riches.*

*As parents and people we have matured in her company.*
*Our horizons have widened immeasureably,*

*Not along the paths we thought we would go*
> *but because she needed constant care we have become self-sufficient, self-centered,*
> *in one sense*
> *but have travelled, explored, sown and harvested, learnt and laboured in a*
> *manner impossible in a 'normal' life.*

*We have experienced all aspects of love —*
*Not just ours for our beloved daughter, but*
*the love hidden away in the worlds of education and healing.*

*Of course there have been shadows across our lives by thoughtlessness and worse*
*Deliberate unkindness, insincerity, insensitivity.*

*But she early taught us the lasting lesson*
> *by her laughter and willingness to meet everyone as a friend*
> *that shadows are only smudges*
> *easily wiped away, leaving no trace.*

*Before meeting Sam people say "Tell me about her"*
*Then when they contact her they say*
*"Even though you love her so your picture was not rich enough". She beggars description.*

*I always want to say to those who have children called handicapped —*
*We must clear our eyes to see what is really there.*
*We should open ourselves to what they offer.*

*Accept the inevitable times of exhaustion, misery and despair —*
*Perhaps you could learn to pray and know insight —*
*But understand they came for a purpose.*
*Not just for us,*
*But for all.*
*One day we may know why.*

> *Meanwhile for me it is enough to sing together*
> *to converse with limited vocabulary (is that so different from most global*
> *dialogue?)*
> *to relish my smile turning to outright laughter at the outrageous impishness*

*the resource of a brain labelled imperfect, but which in truth has depths of
understanding which constantly amazes and delights.*

*Others may be high achievers as we once planned for you.
But I have seen that this was not the path to your incredibly varied and coloured essence.*

*What a task you took on, Sam.
I hope it makes sense to you too, Sam.*

Paddy

Samantha

HOLLY:

My journey with my children began sixteen years ago, when I was living with my mother and my sister in Edinburgh, Scotland in a home for handicapped children. My mother was housemother to ten young people, aged eighteen to twenty-one. I was in the eleventh grade at school. We all lived in one big house, and we were indeed one big family.

After high school I, myself, worked for one year as a housemother to six six-year-old children, in a home for the handicapped in Bristol, England. And then, when I returned to the United States, I worked as a teacher's aide in a special education class, for a short time, before going off to college.

Six years later my daughter Naomi was born. She enriched my life more than words can express. As I began to realize the extent of Naomi's slow development, I vacillated between hope, acceptance and worry. When she was fifteen months old, we took Naomi to a neurologist. He confirmed Naomi's delayed development, but could not tell us why she was delayed, nor could he offer any prognosis. He suggested we wait.

As Naomi grew, it was clear that she was not outgrowing her delays. Yet the extent of the problem, what action we should take, and the reason for those delays was not defined for us. Every friend, relative and professional offered different and conflicting ideas on the subject. I felt totally lost.

Benjamin was born three months shy of Naomi's third birthday. By the time he was six months old, I realized that he, too, was very slow in his development. I tried to ignore it, telling myself that I was overreacting because of Naomi. Yet, I knew. My husband knew, too, but we didn't talk about it. It was just too painful. We weren't ready to deal with it. My paediatrician assured me Benjamin was just fine, so we ignored it... for a while.

Nothing in my experience with disabled children, my love for disabled children, or my studying of children with disabilities, prepared me for the emotional turmoil that I experienced after I knew my children were developmentally delayed.

While doctors and friends were advising me on the special care my children would need, I was left with a headful of information and a heart which was breaking. What my children needed most were their parents. And what their parents needed most was to become whole again. As our children unfolded before us, we began to search for who these little people were, for it was they who held the answers.

Benjamin is now two and one-half years old. He is a curious, happy, unassuming child. His winning smile can charm even the hardest of hearts. Last month he took his first unaided step, and although crawling is still his preferred mode of travel, he is very proud of his new, somewhat shaky, upright stance.

Benjamin speaks no words. His understanding of what I tell him appears quite limited. He is very curious about the things around him, but his ability to manipulate his fingers and hands is still very clumsy. Such skills as feeding himself with a spoon, and potty training, are far off in the future. Benjamin has a keen awareness of others and his gaze is direct and engaging. He is a very sensitive child, and seems to be acutely aware of touch and sound.

The various tests and medical work-ups Benjamin has been through have all proved to be normal. Most doctors have felt that his muscle tone is somewhat hypotonic. The label of cerebral palsy has been tossed around, but the doctors have never felt that cerebral palsy was a truly accurate diagnosis. Although Benjamin is a mystery, his abilities and disabilities are fairly straightforward.

Naomi, although not as delayed as Benjamin, seems much more complicated. At five, she is a strikingly beautiful child, full of joy and wonder for the world around her. There is a naiveté about Naomi which is very appealing to those who come in contact with her. She asks many questions and, indeed, loves to talk. However, she has a difficult time processing the answers to her questions. She often gets stuck, and will repeat the same question over and over again. During these interactions, Naomi is extremely aware of the person with whom she is speaking. She is very interested in their mannerisms, their tone of voice, the mood which surrounds them, and how they are responding and interacting with her.

Naomi has a wide variety of opposite extremes. She is very trusting, on the one hand, yet extremely fearful on the other. She can be perpetual motion – unable to keep still, or a wet, limp noodle who cannot pick herself up off the floor. Naomi can be loving and gentle one moment, and the next moment will strike out and hit or scream. She is unable to play by herself, or with her peers, and is constantly drawing on a grown-up for guidance and limits.

The professionals have offered a variety of speculations concerning Naomi's delayed development. We have been told that she is possibly mildly retarded. We have also been told that she is bright, yet has significant learning disabilities. One doctor feels she has attention deficit disorder. Some of her therapists have felt she has sensory integration dysfunction. Most have felt she has some combination of the above. None are certain. Naomi is too young, they say. Time will tell.

So – it is. I shall wait and watch, and encourage and love my two little children as they unfold before me. My journey is just beginning.

Holly, Jeff, Naomi and Benjamin

Benjamin and Naomi

JENNI:

Our family journey began with a series of crises. Following her birth, Marie was in special care several times, suffering from a series of apparently minor ailments which worsened into life-and-death emergencies. Born with a cleft palate, she couldn't suck properly, and I had to pump my breastmilk for her. She suffered episodes of apnea, where she stopped breathing and turned blue for no reason. She caught a salmonella germ in hospital and lost nearly a third of her birth weight. At one month, Marie didn't blink when a light was flashed in her eyes. Then she didn't smile on time. She didn't wake from hunger. She didn't turn towards a sound. Her cry was a strange piercing yelp. At three months the doctor said, "Your daughter's eyes are normal." The doctor *didn't* say, what she might have said, "It's Marie's brain that is not picking up the nerve impulses properly." Instead the doctor left us to deduce this ourselves.

In due course all the relevant medical tests were performed. Each time the results were given in prudent terms: "Slight abnormality, but within the normal range..." A CT scan done when she was three gave us a diagnosis: congenital hydrocephalus with underdeveloped cerebral cortex and Dandy-Walker Syndrome. The prognosis was grim.

One painful and acute memory remains with me still: "It's double pneumonia," the doctor said. "I don't know if she will make it through the night." I was standing in the hospital corridor, where I had been waiting an interminable time after our four-and-a-half month old Marie, had been rushed into special care. There was nowhere else to wait, so we had waited there, in that bare, neon-lit corridor. It was night. From time to time a group of nurses or doctors went by, chatting as they came off their shift. Occasionally, a late visitor paused for a few moments waiting for the lift to come. For a long time, my husband had gone down to the reception area, to arrange for our daughter's admission. While he was away the doctor came to break the news. His expressionless face and noncommittal manner showed his long familiarity with parents in stress; his only personal remarks were to scold me for still breastfeeding my baby, and for introducing wholemeal baby cereal to her diet. When my husband came back, we were finally allowed a few brief moments with our daughter. She lay uncovered in the hospital cot. Electrodes monitored her breathing and heartbeat. She was blue. I had to argue with a nurse to put socks on her feet; I didn't manage to get a blanket for her.

Eventually, finally, she came home, and I could hold her, wrap and warm her, cuddle her again. And gradually over the next two years we found the help we needed. Marie began physiotherapy, play therapy, music and movement. She has learned to sit up, to stand with support, to grasp an object with help and to feed herself. She enjoys stories and songs. She smiles now in response to adult attention, and often is a keen observer of her brothers' loud games. But Marie remains a beautiful, distant princess, gazing down upon daily affairs from afar. Now attending an excellent school, she is blossoming in the rich programme of music and movement, activities and learning games.

Jenni and Marie

Daniel's birth was quick and easy. He was a big, beautiful baby. But... he didn't want to feed, and he was too sleepy. In fact, he was acting like a premature baby, or a baby with brain dysfunction. Through my experiences with Marie, I recognised the abnormal signs within a day of his birth. The verdict was undeniable: if he is sleepy, he should at least suck when he is hungry; or if he cannot suck, he should at least be waking from hunger. But if he is both too sleepy *and* cannot suck, then he has a significant neurological problem. The first three months were a total nightmare. I knew something was very wrong, and I tried frantically to get my friends and family, doctors and other professionals to recognize what to me was so obvious. The worst was that Daniel showed the same signs of autism that Marie showed; no eye contact, (though the eye doctor declared Daniel's eyes to be normal), dislike of being held, few smiles. There were no emergencies, just a dark gray fog around us.

As luck would have it, my husband got a new job in Gloucester. Our move to England was a turning point for the entire family. Within two months, we had seen a series of very helpful professionals – physios, speech therapists, specialist doctors – and both Marie and Daniel were enrolled into excellent learning programmes. Three years later Daniel is now walking with minimal support, beginning to speak, and generally being a chubby, cheeky, happy toddler. Though still significantly behind, Daniel's progress has been almost miraculous.

My way of coping through these past few years has been by talking – first with friends in similar situations, later with professional therapists. I needed to explore in many directions, some directly concerned with the children, others leading to many other life experiences. The more I have looked at my own life story, the more I have realized two things. First, that the children's handicaps are not really the "problem" that I had first thought. The "problems" came from my own fears, prejudices, expectations and need for gratifications. And second, as I have gradually confronted these, I have been able to see each child as a whole person, accepting each one individually, beyond my wishes or desires of how they might have been. As this sense of each child's inner being has dawned in me, I have felt my own feelings recede. I have felt a deepening sense of the tragedies of human life in general. The children have carved out in my heart a new dimension, a new capacity to grasp human suffering.

With this has come, gradually at first, then in great waves, a terrific gratitude for the blessings in life – for my own health, the richness of the senses, for our home and marriage, for my education which enables me to advocate for our children. Sometimes, when I am able to clear my soul sufficiently of the debris of stress and clutter of an active life, I am filled with a joy in Creation, a wonder at human life, and awe in the miracles of the universe. This dawning of joy in no way diminishes the stress of daily life, the grief, pain or anger at bearing the burdens. Rather, it begins to dawn *through* these, around and beyond these, putting them into perspective and filling them with a sense of deeper meaning. In honesty, I am not yet at peace, nor have I reached the serenity of the saints. I am still, and expect to remain, with my feet in the mud and my mind preoccupied with daily living. My goals have become simpler; a little more patience with the hassles of life, a little more readiness to celebrate life's small beauties and achievements.

HELEN:

The time surrounding my pregnancy and the birth of our first child, Keziah, was an intensely emotional one and our relationship broke up temporarily. However, from the moment of her birth to this day, our relationship and that with Keziah, goes from strength to strength. It may be that the fact of Keziah's handicap has brought us closer and enabled us to give the everyday emotional support that is so necessary.

Keziah is just five. She has short brown wavy hair that frames an invariably smiling face. Everyone who meets her comments on her beautiful eyes, which have long lashes and shine wonderfully.

Keziah has cerebral palsy and was probably somehow affected during pregnancy, as there was no physical trauma around the birth. All four of her limbs are severely affected, her arms more than her legs, and she is as yet unable to use any of her limbs purposefully. Her jaw too is affected giving her the well known spastic 'gape' which can deter strangers. Her jaw and throat spasm mean that her breathing is mostly by mouth and can be noisy, feeding her and giving her drinks is a challenge and speech unlikely. As with all her limbs, the more she tries, the more spasm there is. When she attempts to vocalize, it becomes more difficult for sound to emerge. Show her a chocolate digestive and she tries very hard!

Keziah has a wonderful nature which makes loving her deeply very easy, even when constant daily demands strain one's short-term patience and equanimity. She smiles readily, watches closely everything that goes on between people and has an infectious chuckling laugh, particularly appreciating other people's clumsiness. What an irony! She is always willing to 'make friends' with someone new and to get them to pay her attention. She is usually successful, once even on the underground at rush hour when she bored through someone's newspaper until her 'subject' looked up. Yet her short attention span seriously detracts from all efforts to encourage her to communicate, for example – choice making, which in time could lead to pointing at symbols as a method of communication. If Keziah is shown a choice of two drinks, it is very hard to tell which one she would prefer. She will look at one and then the other and then all around the room. Perhaps more than any one other thing, I would love Keziah to be able to tell us, somehow, what she wants.

I was anxious on Keziah's behalf that she would be upset when her little brother (Fred, born just before her third birthday) was able to play and move independently. She shows no signs of grief or envy at all, and dearly loves him.

After five years, I think we have come a long way in accepting Keziah's handicap; I'm not sure that anyone fully accepts it. Who does not wish for it all to be different? Finding ease in the way things are is always the first step towards peace in any struggle. With Keziah there is not the feedback that a normal child gives. We must learn to read signals and see what is not so obvious. Having a handicapped child also means facing up to one's expectations of how a child 'should' be and understanding that here is a special individual who poses particularly searching questions to his or her parents. One is asked to take a challenging and twisting path which scales the peaks of happiness, unadulterated by *why?* or *what if?* and plunges to valleys of darkness and desperation. Keziah is the loving teacher and guide on this journey and we are simply the sometimes reluctant and often ungrateful pupils.

Keziah and Helen

Why my child?

# 3

## *Why My Child?*

HOLLY:

"Why me?" is one of the first questions we ask ourselves when we learn our child is, in some way, fundamentally different from other children. This is obviously not a usual occurrence. Otherwise, our child would be accepted as 'normal'. "Of all the people in the world, why am I the parent of this special child?" we ask. Soon we begin to alternate this question with, "Why my child?" Growing up is difficult enough for a young child when he has everything going for him. Why would anyone want to make it harder?

For me, the final answers to these questions were not as important as the searching for the answers. I thought that the answers would make the pain go away. As I look back, I realize it was the searching which healed. By virtue of seeking for an answer, I realized that I had something to learn. "What is it that I want to learn?" "Whom do I ask?" "Where do I go to learn it?" Some may turn to science for answers. Others to religion. Still others to psychology. Ultimately, I found the answer was in front of me all along. The answer lay in my child.

Gradually, I began to observe my child by placing myself inside him. I tried to imagine how the world looked and felt from where he was. What did he perceive from his environment and from those around him? What did he bring to the world? What was our relationship? What was it that lived between him and me?

By exploring these questions, I discovered many answers. The knowledge I gained is nothing I could have learned in a book or a lecture. It is unique to me. It is a knowledge I cannot always articulate. It seems that whenever I try, no words can explain what I feel. All children are indeed a mystery. I often look at my children as having the same problems as normal children have, yet magnified a hundredfold.

I believe that it would be extraordinarily beneficial if all parents of disabled or normal children would ask themselves these questions about their child. For parents of normal children, such questions are not essential for their daily existence. However, I think parents who don't ask those questions lose a great deal. And they don't even know it.

Why my child? Others can help to provide part of the answer, but only we can lay the foundation by really knowing our child.

PADDY:

Truthfully, at no time during my life with Sam, have I ever asked myself the question: "Why my child?" though on occasion I have been questioned quite deeply about it. The first time it was put to me I remember being amazed, for I have loved Sam every moment of our time together and even throughout the pregnancy (a miserable time for I was ill most of it) I thought about the things we would do together.

When the little pink bundle was put into my arms for the first time I still recall the surge of love for her so strong it had the impact of a physical blow. As I gradually realised her problems, their magnitude and her vulnerability, I loved her even more and felt enormously protective. Being a Mother means helping the child through all its difficulties, whatever they are, surely?

Long before marriage, when I was teaching, I found it most rewarding to teach pupils who had difficulties in learning, those at the bottom of the heap, as it were and eventually acquired specialisations in this area, so clearly something has always drawn me towards those with these needs.

I am so glad Sam came to us. We cannot all be perfect – the thought of her not having the love, attention and my will to fight for her (and others like her) concerns me and fosters my courage. Of course, I would not have chosen for her to be handicapped nor chosen to have my life thus constricted, so exhausting, daunting, sad and in many ways unfulfilled, but she is worth all the efforts and the reward has been to see her come alive. I have immense pride in her efforts to be part of the world and her zest for life for she has had to strive to make tiny gains all her life.

"Does she understand and appreciate this?" is the next question, of course. Well, she loves her Ma and Pa devotedly: we are her whole life for we are in a sense her conductors. On the surface and at her developmental stage I doubt she realises how her presence has affected our lives but she is completely confident in our love for her and rightly so. She takes us for granted and is completely self-centered but I feel she will grow beyond this.

However, I am often aware that at another level Sam understands our sacrifice and our wholehearted acceptance of the task. When she achieves some step forward which delights her she looks to us for praise, and as we hug and applaud we three share a deep, unspoken tribute to her efforts and our efforts. And when she grins contentedly and whispers "I love you" as she drops off to sleep there is adult understanding there, too.

Likewise, when she is mischievous or naughty (and that happens quite often too), perhaps deliberately damages something (if I don't get there in time!) then that is part of our relationship also and we can be a little cross with each other, though this doesn't last long and is part of discovering about each other's world and another step in the right direction.

So perhaps the reason for the question "Why me?" is that I have always sought out a challenge. I have certainly found an enthralling one with Sam.

JENNI:

There seem to be stages which many parents go through in the process of accepting the arrival of a child with handicap – grief, rage, guilt, despair – until some degree of acceptance grows, and the parents learn to cope with the situation. In our case, we went through this process twice, with the birth of each of our two children with handicap. Each time, the process was different. With our daughter Marie, our first born, I felt, and still feel, a tremendous sense of guilt. Through professional counselling help I have gradually been able to sort out the feelings which directly relate to Marie, from those which relate to earlier relationships in my life. I have also felt much grief, partly due to a sense of Marie's loss of opportunities, but largely due to the projection of my life as a woman, upon her potential life as a baby girl, and all the ways in which I had hoped she would be more successful than I, or more 'fulfilled' as a woman.

When our third child, Daniel, was also born with handicap, I felt much greater despair and loss than I had with Marie. Marie's frequent hospitalizations gave a sense of emergency which buoyed me up and gave my life purpose and meaning. With Daniel, there were no emergencies, only the dreaded daily

reality of his 'backwardness'. By this I mean, the mass of evidence showing that
he was *not* developing and responding as he should have been. We already had
our middle child, Patrick, then an energetic two-year-old. He wanted a little
brother to play with. So the grief I felt after Daniel's birth was grief about
*Patrick's* loss of a "dream younger brother". As it turns out, Daniel has developed exceedingly well, he and Patrick *do* play well together now, and Patrick never
seems to have felt any grief himself. This has helped heal my own grief
tremendously.

The despair experienced after Daniel's birth forced me to think more carefully
and, I hope, more profoundly, about the question of destiny, and why these
children had been born to us. While we had only one child with handicap, my
main feelings about it concerned why it had happened to *us*. It seemed a personal
affront, a kind of huge burden that life had prepared especially for our frail
shoulders. All I could see around me were other people's 'perfect' children.
When I did occasionally meet a family with a child worse off than ours, my mind
just could not take it in. I was sure that our burden was the heaviest, our
daughter the most afflicted.

During the pregnancy with Marie I had vague feelings of uneasiness, and
some dreams which indicated something might be wrong. But I put those down
to the nervousness of a first-time mother. During the pregnancy with Daniel, I
had much stronger intuitive feelings of his handicap, and this time I didn't
dismiss them, because by then I had learned to accept the reality of "mother's
intuition". (This has since been confirmed many times hearing other mothers'
stories.) However, I was still just as unprepared for the shock as I had been the
first time. Later, when a leading paediatric neurologist said to us, "In my 30
years of medical practice, I have never seen a family like yours," I knew I would
have to start looking on another level than the purely medical or personal, if I
wanted to make some sense out of why this had happened to us.

One day, I was standing waiting to cross the street in a bustling shopping area.
I was feeling particularly dreadful that morning, and the bright sunshine and
throngs of people around me only made me feel worse and more alienated.
Suddenly it came to me that I had a *choice* about how I wore my "cloak of grief".
Life and Creation all around me wanted to see me smiling, and not hiding
behind a wall of darkness. I realized that I had a duty to make a step forward, to
try to look upwards and outwards, and to appreciate the beauty of life about me.
Only in making such small steps would I be of any use at all to this flow of life,

and certainly I would be no use at all, but a bigger burden, if I doggedly continued to carry this "cloak" around me, as an excuse to avoid growth. I did *not* suddenly feel healed, nor were my "burdens miraculously lifted". Rather, I began to sense the difference between the intense feelings which well up spontaneously, and the mass of *old* grief I was clinging to. So, standing on that street corner, I inwardly made a step away from grief towards the celebration of life. I also grasped that by feeling that my problems were the worst ones, and that "Life was out to get me," I was in fact being terribly egocentric. I mean, who am *I* so important that life should be out just to "get" *me*?!

Another key moment was a conversation with my husband's beloved uncle, a Catholic priest. I was throwing at him comments like "How can there be a loving God if He can allow such tragedy?" and "Why is God testing us, anyway?" Without reacting to my anger, he simply shared with me his fervent conviction that God *is* present, not to take us *away* from the trials of life, but to *accompany* us through them. He spoke of the Now-ness of God, of the healing power of the Spirit, despite, through, and beyond the sufferings of the body. From that conversation I gained a sense of healing, and glimpsed the presence of a God so great that all Creation, all pain, and all suffering are "held within his hand".

Books have been a great help to me as well. I have devoured as many biographies as I could find, both of "great" people of history, and of people with handicaps. Looking at the patterns in the lives of others has helped me to sense some patterns in my own life. Often people seem to come to a moment of choice in life, sometimes of great crisis, and frequently it comes when they feel least able to choose clearly. When they do choose to *do* that which beckons – whether to stand up for their beliefs, (even to the point of martyrdom,) to begin a new career, or to commit themselves to a cause or an inner path, perhaps even taking a vow – then their lives begin to resonate with new meaning, and they find the strength and purpose to carry on.

Another source of strength has been the example of such people as Jean Vannier and Marie-Hélène Matthieu of the journal *Ombres et Lumière*, part of the Faith and Light movement in the Catholic church. They have done a great deal of work to raise people's consciousness about the dignity of people with handicaps. For them, the person who has a handicap, through his or her utter mental or physical poverty of expression, is the living presence of the Divine amongst us. This meditation on humility and service towards others has helped me a great deal.

I have also found it meaningful to read international news magazines. When I read about the problems in the Third World, the on-going struggles for political freedom in so many countries, the immensity of suffering in this world due to human greed, prejudice and powerlust, our family's problems fall into perspective, and I realize how lucky we are in the gifts we have been given; and also that we have a duty to "be part of the solution" to world problems. This may be in tiny ways – even just by thinking positive thoughts about disaster spots in the current news – or it might lead to positive action, either in the local community or in a larger context. There are many ways to help. For me what counts is realizing that "my family" is really the "human family," and it is both urgent, and meaningful to widen my area of concern, even if only in thought, to include the whole world.

Grief

# 4

# *Grief*

JENNI:

One of the first, and certainly one of the longest-lasting, feelings parents of children with handicaps experience, is grief. It has manifold aspects, and will be felt in varying ways by different individuals. There is an acute sense of loss, both present and future. Our child is not 'normal': he doesn't have nice features, perfect fingers, pretty eyes, luxurious hair; our child drools, thrusts out her tongue, makes grimaces, rolls her eyes or other 'revolting', "socially un-acceptable" behaviour.

*Our child is not keeping up with the others:* we're on the "outside" looking into the club of "normal" people; the girl next door is walking already, our child can't sit up; the boy around the block is in Scouts, our boy is still in nappies; the boss's daughter is getting married, our daughter is in a "special home".

*Normal family relationships are lost:* "He'll never be able to play cowboys with his brother"; "she'll never help Gran in the garden;" he'll never be able to play football with Dad"; "we'll never see her a bride"; "we'll never have grand-children..." Our child may die early, or remain totally dependent all her life.

We grieve because our child may be in pain, whether physical, emotional, or spiritual. We see the child's pain and feel it as our own but cannot take it from him nor, beyond a point, protect him from it. Here arises part of our rage at doctors and hospitals whom we perceive as *inflicting* pain on our child, against our will. The child may realize he isn't 'normal' and may himself suffer feelings of rejection, inferiority, despair, hopelessness, anger, etc. A child with normal intelligence, but a physical or sensory handicap may be struggling with terrible feelings of rage, grief or loss, and may be in danger of losing a sense of meaning in life. We may mourn our own loss of faith. How could a loving God allow this to happen? Where is God's light now that I'm in darkness? What sin have I committed that God did this to my child? etc.

People may make inept, unkind remarks. There may be a sense of loss of social standing: What will the neighbours, relatives, work colleagues, social worker, teachers, supermarket cashier, shoe salesman,... think of us?

How do I stand up in public and say "This is my child. My child is handicapped, imperfect, not beautiful, anti-social,... but *still my child*"?

Depending on the benefits available to us and the country we live in, we may find that "doing right by our child" costs us a tremendous amount of money for therapies, transportation, special equipment, medical expenses, health-care and sanitary products, etc. Family finances may also be set back by the need to hire help into the home, babysitting and respite care fees; also family wage earners may be hampered in their job advancement through lack of extra time or availability due to family commitments.

There will be a feeling of loss of opportunities: *Where we go together* as a family becomes restricted by *access,* in a physical sense – we can no longer walk along country pathways, go up long stairs, explore narrow climbing lanes in little villages, many public places and museums are still limited access – and restricted by *acceptance* in an emotional sense – will our child's behaviour, looks, manner, be accepted graciously in restaurants, concert halls, public transportation, shops and department stores...?

Finally, for many parents there is an inarticulate, existential form of grief: the on-going experience of painful feelings in our personal lives may make us feel especially vulnerable to the suffering of others that we hear about through friends, the media or thinking about recent world history. The news of terrible suffering in the world reaches us constantly from many sources, and we may find ourselves grieving for others' pain and for the state the world is in. "Selbstschmerz" (self pain) becomes "Weltschmerz" (existential pain).

HOLLY:

As Benjamin grew, so did the small pain of dreaded knowledge that something was not right. Every time I brought up my concerns to professionals or friends, they shrugged it off and told me to wait. I waited. Perhaps it would go away if I waited long enough.

One day, when Benjamin was nine months old, I mentioned to an acquaintance that I had some questions about his development. She suggested I visit a special program. Even before I got there, I knew they would confirm my suspicions. I was finally facing it; I couldn't deny it any longer. Benjamin was not the normal bouncing baby I had planned to have.

I couldn't believe this was happening to me a second time. Hadn't I already paid my dues with Naomi? All my friends had two, three or four normal children, with not one disabled child among them. Where was the angel that made the mistake and gave me two? I was angry. I was bitter. I was overwhelmed with grief. I was trying to escape from the island God had put me on and I was drowning.

The tutor that came to help Benjamin every week couldn't hide her alarm at all the things Benjamin couldn't do. The doctors, and the applications I had to fill out to apply for funding, focused on the lack of Benjamin's achievements. I felt as if my baby were being reduced from a person to a nothing.

Even in the infant stimulation group where Benjamin now went for therapy, with five other disabled children, he gradually slipped into a tie for last place as other children surpassed him in their development.

I was enveloped in unknowns. Would my baby catch up? Would he be retarded? Would he move like a normal person? What kind of life would he have? What kind of life would I have? Would he ever be able to live on his own? Would I ever be a grandmother? The list was endless.

I remember the times when waves of grief would wash over me, taking any strength and happiness I had, and washing it out to sea. I couldn't always predict when the waves would come. They would always come when I saw other babies his age, but sometimes they would come when I was watching him in his beautiful contentedness. I would cry until I thought my heart would break.

I handled my grief in relative isolation. I was like an open wound and I didn't want anyone touching me with their thoughts. Like any wound, time was the best healer.

Eventually, I joined two support groups for parents of special children. These groups were invaluable to the healing process and the road to accepting the new life I was to have. These parents knew first-hand what I was going through. They told me it was all right to grieve. It was even normal that I was drowning. They jumped in with me and helped teach me to swim.

As I began to gain some perspective on life, I began to understand that there are two aspects to learning to accept a child with special needs. The first hurdle is accepting this unique human being. The second, more difficult task, is feeling comfortable with the effects it will have upon your life. For example, perhaps I study ten years to be a surgeon, and then develop tremors in my hands. I must learn to accept that these tremors are now a part of me. I must also accept the change that comes about in my daily life as a result of this unexpected development.

The grief is gone now. My feelings of sadness are usually directed to more external things: the doctor who thinks my observations are irrelevant, or the friend who looks at Benjamin with pity. My children's future is still unknown. The path ahead of me is still unpaved. Yet I am becoming accustomed to this. In its unfamiliarity it is becoming familiar.

JENNI:

For those coping with feelings of grief and its aftermath of depression, I would offer the following suggestions. In all humility, I know how devastating grief can be. Firstly, try to remember that there can be great dignity in grief and that by allowing youself to grieve fully you may go a long way towards healing of the wounds. Secondly, look after yourself. Eating properly and getting enough sleep can help tremendously by giving one strength to face the emotional pain. Thirdly, find a book on the subject of grieving: bookshops and libraries always carry a number of helpful books on the subject. Fourthly, seek professional help if you feel you are "going under" and can't find a sympathetic ear – family guidance clinics, a local clergy person or the Samaritans would be a good place to start. And lastly, try not to cling to your grief through a kind of morbid going-over-and-over of events or feelings – let your feelings heal over when the time is right – you'll find that gradually life does become livable again, and is calling to each of us to live it to the full.

Guilt

# 5

# *Guilt*

JENNI:

Unlike grief, which can often be outwardly expressed and often feels inwardly justified, guilt can be a "sneaky", "sly" feeling which guides our choices and actions without our conscious knowledge. Even people who have children with no handicaps find themselves acting or reacting out of a sense of guilt. So much more so for us parents, especially as often we can do little to change the situation we feel guilty about. If we feel guilty about the past, that certainly can't be changed; and if we feel guilty about not meeting our child's needs, his perceived miserableness or lack of lovable qualities, our guilt may in fact be an objective appraisal of the situation; our child may indeed be miserable, need more stimulation, be behaving in an obnoxious, unlovable way, etc. What we can change, however, is *what we do about our guilty feelings*.

One first step is to acknowledge to ourselves *what* we feel guilty about, writing down a list if necessary. A second step might be to try to disentangle our guilt feelings from anger, i.e., "I feel guilty for not stimulating my child every minute of the day, but I am also resentful at having to spend so much time stimulating him anyway!" or other similar thoughts. Thirdly, if we listen to parents of "normal" children, we may indeed hear a lot of similar feelings coming out, and this can help us relativize our child's handicap, and realize that our guilty feelings may have more to do with being "imperfect" parents than with the actual handicap itself. This can help a lot!

We may feel guilty because of:

– What we did/thought/felt during pregnancy. Perhaps we were ambivalent about the pregnancy in the first place?

– Any things we may have done *before* the pregnancy (Different partners? Dangerous sports? Smoking, drinking or drug use? Not following our doctor's "orders"?...) or things we have done *since* the birth (any of the above, plus feelings we have had, lack of experience in caring for a new-born, etc...)

– Our anger at our own parents for how they raised us, what they are currently demanding of us, how we behaved during our adolescent "rebellion" and what we may have "done" to our own parents then...

– Not "loving" our child enough, (i.e. feeling sympathy and warmth) for our child who may be screaming, dirty, ugly, dependent on us, smelly, remote and unresponsive, passive, who has "caused us this distress in the first place"...

– Not meeting our child's needs (as we perceive them) "perfectly"...

– Not "stimulating" our child every minute of the day...

– Going out somewhere *without* the child...

– Wishing our child were dead (or had not been born, or had died in infancy)...

– Being ourselves happy when our child "is so miserable"...

– Not presenting our husband/wife/parents/friends with a perfect/beautiful/ intelligent/performing child...

– Hating God (will He strike us down with a thunderbolt?)

– Not celebrating our child's life as we would with a normal child (birthdays which go by forgotten, no baby book, few photos, no holidays, etc.)

– Receiving financial benefits from the government (we may know people whose lives are as stressful as our own but whose "handicaps" don't qualify for benefits, such as alcoholism, lack of education, social deprivation and lack of opportunities, etc.) and *we* are receiving money that might have helped *their* lives get better).

If such thoughts or feelings do exist, they will need to be acknowledged and/or "talked through" before they will go away. You may find that you can deal with this yourself; that "time heals".

If not, if guilt becomes overwhelming in your personal life, do seek out a family guidance counsellor, clergy-person or health-care professional. Sometimes intangible pain warrants treatment and help, just as much as physical cuts or bruises do.

HOLLY:

Guilt is possibly the strongest emotion the parent of a child with an undiagnosed problem has. I didn't feel guilty for things I did, so much as for things I didn't do. Did I not play with them enough? Sing to them enough? Talk to them enough?

I felt guilty about feelings I had. Surely these are two very special little people who need my love, my care, my job and my respect in order to develop to their fullest potential. I shouldn't feel sad or disappointed that they aren't normal. After all, for all anyone knew my children might grow up to be "normal!". And then I would feel guilty about not having enough faith.

Every doctor and every therapist my children saw gave me much credit for how I loved and encouraged my children. Still, I couldn't hear it. I thought these professionals didn't really know me.

Although consciously I knew better, subconsciously I thought there was a direct correlation between what I did, and how much my child would achieve. This is a prevalent feeling in our society. Of course, we parents can have great influence on our children. All children come into the world with their own gifts and their own shortcomings. But we cannot create what they don't have. It is one thing to know this intellectually, another to know it in your heart, and still another to put it into practice. In order to put it into practice, one must first enter into who the child is. We must not confuse who he is with how we think he should be.

Once I was able to know this in my heart, and put it into practice, I was also able to let go of my guilt.

PADDY:

When Sam was three a friend said "You know you are supposed to feel guilt" – which was a completely new idea to me – and since she said it with half a smile I knew she realised this. If as a parent you feel guilt then you have to deal with it. For myself it was more helpful to the situation to face it and then forget it.

What I did feel was sadness though as we've gone along together. Sadness that Sam could not react to toys lovingly given by my friends, sadness always that she had no friends, sadness when she runs to play on swings (which she loves) and other kids move away and stare silently.

I've been sad too that we couldn't share things like a good book or a concert and that our family life is curtailed. But realise that many parents don't receive the expected relationships they thought would emerge as their youngster grew up.

What I see as unfortunate about this suggestion of 'guilt' is that parents of handicapped people are often put into defensive positions by society – guilt that they are responsible for a 'burden' to themselves and society, an attitude becoming increasingly evident nowadays. Thus I accept sadness, knowing the joys too and trusting that society will gradually become more aware and more generous.

Marriage and partnership

# 6

## *Marriage and Partnership*

HOLLY:

I think that marriage has much to do with balance. It has to do with giving and receiving, with being as one whole, yet maintaining one's own individuality. Marriage involves feelings of love and feelings of anger, of hope and of disappointment, of happiness and of sadness.

When we first got married, my husband and I found the right balance belonging to us through trial and error. As changes in our life occurred, our equilibrium would be challenged, and a new balance would be established. Some changes were easy to accommodate. Others were more difficult. The growing knowledge that our two children were going to need a great deal of special care, tipped our comfortable balance considerably. Perhaps any trauma would. As we found ourselves slipping into a completely unknown, unplanned and unwanted situation, we were forced to grow. New struggles and feelings were awakened. We struggled with new discoveries about ourselves, our values and our goals.

Jeff became increasingly involved in his work – working seventy to eighty hours over six to six and one-half days per week. I read books, researched, and completely involved myself with what was going on with our children. We were lucky in that our philosophy about life, our ultimate goals for our family, and the values which we held were common to one another. Yet our lives were very separate.

I felt abandoned by Jeff. The labor involved in caring for my children was tremendous. I took my children to ten therapy sessions per week, plus worked on the exercises the therapists gave, at home. What most children pick up routinely as they grow, my children needed to be taught, and with a great deal of patience, repetitiveness and love. It took an enormous amount of time and energy dealing with the doctors, as well as the agencies where I applied for financial assistance for the children's medical bills. On top of this, I carried out the responsibilities of most other home-makers: cooking, cleaning, shopping, bookkeeping and the myriad other activities involved in family life.

Jeff's job, as a class teacher in a Waldorf school, involves a tremendous amount of preparation, study and meetings. The job is both emotionally and intellectually demanding. Jeff and I have had to work hard in order to find the right balance between Jeff's work, my work, time for us as a couple, and time for our family as a whole.

Communication is essential. In our busy lives it is easy to feel we don't have time to sit down over coffee, *without* children and talk. Jeff and I find we must write it in our daily schedule, or it slips right by us. We put our children to bed at 7:00 every evening. From 7:30 to 8:00 we linger over ice-cream and discuss whatever is on our minds. It gives us a chance to work on minor difficulties, plan our schedules and share our news and concerns. If our communication time needs longer, we take it. If a meeting or event gets in the way, we know we shall have time to share the next day. Of course, some issues can't wait. But we have found that most can.

Soon after Naomi was born, when babysitters and finances were hardest, Jeff and I developed an alternative to dinner out. We eat dinner at home, but with a difference. We invest in an entrée that is very special, but easy to make or reheat. After we put the children to bed at 7:00, we change in to going–out clothes. We put on a nice record, turn out the lights, and light candles all around. We then sit down to a beautifully set table and eat in the glow of it all.

Depending upon what we are eating, and the music we put on, we create a French, or Greek or Italian atmosphere. After dinner, we retire to our living room cafe for dessert, coffee and more conversation. The dishes and clean–up wait till morning. We like this so much that we still continue to do it.

We also try to get out about once a month for dinner, a movie, folk dancing or something just for fun, to remind us that underneath all the stress and hard work, we love each other.

Sharing the responsibility of parenting our two special children is our most difficult challenge. Finding the right balance has not been an easy task. It is something we are constantly re-negotiating as the children's, Jeff's or my needs change. We have not arrived at any clear solution how best to do this.

Having children with special needs is indeed a challenge to any marriage. Each parent deals with the turmoil and confusion in a different way. Each overcomes the initial devastation in his own time. A metamorphosis takes place for each parent separately. Some couples grow apart. Others are brought closer together. No marriage is left unchanged.

JENNI:

In our marriage we have found that having children with handicaps has both exaggerated all the weaknesses and strains, as well as re-inforced the strengths and sharing. The marriage is certainly put under more stress, outwardly because of the difficulties in our daily life, and inwardly because of having to cope with our feelings about our children. My husband and I have dealt with our feelings quite differently, he being more introverted and I more extroverted in our personalities. At times the pace of our acceptance has been different. With our daughter he seemed to accept the fact of her handicaps earlier and more easily than I did; with our son, I recognised the signs earlier and seemed to "face up" more quickly than he did. We have needed to show each other a lot of tolerance, and not expect the other person to be feeling exactly the same thing at the same time. From the very beginning my husband has shared equally all aspects of child-care, which has both helped him to bond deeply with the children, and helped lessen my workload considerably. Over the years we have both begun to recognise the other's "emotional danger signals," which helps us to make allowances for each other, or be a little bit more understanding. Of course there have often been times that we were *both* feeling depressed or angry or tired. In that case we generally put the kids in the car and go out for a walk in nature somewhere. Fresh air seems to help us the most in those situations. We have tried to do little things for each other that show we still remember each other "before" our lives were turned upside-down – cups of tea in the morning, little gifts on Mother's and Father's day, dinner out on our anniversary, etc.

Very early we realised we would need to get out together regularly, at least once a week. We have had a series of long-term baby-sitters, usually a local teenager, who would come to us on a certain night every week. This has made it possible for us to sing in a choir, which we have found to be very restorative. We have also had reciprocal baby-sitting arrangements with other families. Even babysitting for the other family has seemed relaxing at times! In the last two years we have arranged to go away by ourselves at least one weekend every few months. Generally we have distributed the children amongst friends, although a few times we have asked friends with no children of their own to come and stay with our children at our house. That is certainly the easiest solution on a practical level. Our social worker has also helped us to apply for available respite care in our local community.

On our wedding anniversary and during our summer holidays, we try to look back on the year just past, and look forward to the year to come. Doing this on a quiet evening away from the children, has helped us to see how we might do things differently or organise ourselves better to cope with daily life. We have found the beginning of a new school year is a good time to make changes in our daily routines, along with the changes that naturally come from work and school at that time of year.

We have made a conscious effort to take up activities again that we enjoyed before the children were born. Though this has meant having to confront some feelings of guilt about "leaving the children behind," I believe it has really helped the whole family, because we are happier and less stressed now that some of our own needs are also being met.

From time to time each of us has also gone away alone for a day or two, either to attend a workshop or conference or to make a retreat to a place of spiritual quiet. This has helped us individually to take stock of our lives, consider choices and changes, or simply be quiet, utterly quiet. During that time we ask a friend or family member to come and stay at the house with the spouse at home, so that there will be no extra work or stress over-load to cope with.

Finally, it has helped us a lot that we both believe in marriage, in the strength of our mutual commitment, in the value of working hard for what we have. I pray that we may continue to find the strength which has thus far helped us to stay together and experience together our unique family life.

Going it alone

# 7

## *Going It Alone*

MANDY:

I didn't choose to be a single parent; in fact, my pregnancy at age seventeen was what you could call a silly mistake. But I was three and a half months along before I was really certain, and when the doctor told me how formed the baby in my womb was already, I couldn't face an abortion. In fact, Katy was born prematurely, weighed only 3lb 11oz at birth and needed to stay in hospital six weeks before she could come home. She seemed fine, a little bit late in her development, but she babbled, played with toys and crawled. She had a squint, and an operation at about one year old for this. It was after the operation that things started going wrong. The few words Katy had known –"Mum," "Dad", "Up" disappeared. She would no longer handle toys or play normally. We started trips to doctors and tests of different kinds.

Katy and I were still living at home with Mum and Dad during that time of uncertainty. My sister and I shared a room along with the baby which could be difficult at night when Katy was wakeful. But they were all very supportive, and still are.

Eventually Katy was diagnosed as being autistic. Coming to terms with this was terrible. I'd keep talking to her as though she was perfectly normal, not really wanting anyone to know, at first. If she was kicking or screaming in the pushchair, I'd tell people she was over-tired, make excuses, and then go home and cry. The specialists used such big, baffling words; I was confused as well as depressed about it all. But the family doctor put me in touch with the Spring Centre in Gloucester, a place where parents and their special children can meet, play, talk and share. This helped enormously, especially before Katy was in school.

I've got my own home now, with a bedroom for myself and a bedroom for

Katy. These rooms are very important for identity and privacy. Katy's is done up really nicely, is safe for her, and she seems to love it. If she's wakeful at night I know she can play or sit there (she'll sometimes stand and gaze out the window) safely until she goes off to sleep again. If her behaviour gets really out-of-hand in the day, with non-stop screaming or thrashing, I sometimes simply put her in her room and she can carry on until she is finished. It's better that way for both of us. Being a single parent and a single child, we must create some kind of space between us sometimes or everything would become too intense.

When we moved in, I explained to the neighbours what our situation is, and they've been very good. The local people and shopkeepers know Katie and say "hello" – it's really been up to me to feel brave enough to go out and meet people. Once they know us, people are generally fine.

At four years old Katy is in school now. As I don't have transport and school is a fair distance away, a taxi calls for Katy at 8:30 each morning and brings her home again. There is a special little book she takes to and from school with her each day with messages from me to the teachers or vice versa. For example, if she's had a dreadful night, I can let them know that she might be tired today. If she's done something special in class I'll have a note to tell me so that I can share that with her in the evening. This way I feel in close contact with Katy's school life even though I don't actually go there each day. It is a stable and secure school situation for Katy and it frees me in the day to have time for other things.

People say I must have a lot of patience, but I don't know if I do. I just believe in getting on with things. All my daughter does is run around the house and clap her hands. She will hold a cup for herself sometimes only if she is terribly thirsty. Usually drinks and food go to the floor if she is not helped. She needs clean pyjamas and sheets every day, in spite of large size nappies, and there is a lot of cleaning up to do. She's heavy for me to carry now, and often refuses to crawl up the stairs. So I make it a game, calling her from above, but always watching that she doesn't fall. We do laugh a lot together, and she giggles if I say "Boo". She likes books and musical toys but doesn't "play" in any conventional sense with other things. On weekends or during school holidays we are best outdoors. She loves running along in a garden, clapping her hands. I can walk her to the shops, but it is very slow going. Depending on the weather and her mood, we have our good days and bad days. Sometimes we need to sit quietly together for ten minutes or more, just to get back in touch with each other.

Any person in my position needs to find people they can trust, and then trust them sometimes for help. I'm twenty-one years old now, and I'll be a better mother to Katy if I keep developing as a person, myself. There is a lot in life ahead for both of us! I do get a baby sitter sometimes in the evenings, when she's asleep – people she would know if she should wake up – and I do keep up my appearance and interests and go out sometimes. I have a boyfriend who knows and understands about Katy. I think he even understands that on some days when she's been really naughty I take it out on him!

If you are on your own, remind yourself that most parents probably feel "trapped" at some time. If you can get through a bad day, the next one may be much better. Check out local respite schemes, find what you feel is right, and use it. I've just discovered a "Handi-care" organization in which people take children like Katy to relieve parents for a while if they need it. It could mean a whole day out, or even a weekend away for me, providing Katy felt at ease and the people seem right. We are both young, she and I, the long-term future is uncertain, and I take each day for what it is.

When my little girl is very tired or really upset and needing me she will still say "Mum". These are moments of closeness, and I can hope that one day she will say more things again. Meanwhile, it is one step at a time.

Friends

# 8
## *Friends*

HELEN:

It can be very lonely having a handicapped child and I do not think we could manage without the love and support of each other. One thing that recurs is what we see as a lack of real insight by most people into how it is to live with Kezzie. Not in the daily round of care and attendance but what it takes emotionally – to listen to people talking, apparently without thinking, of children growing up and becoming independent; seeing other 5-year-olds running, playing, skipping, always being on call.

HOLLY:

When I learned that not only my daughter, but also my son, was developmentally delayed, I felt as if I had been thrust onto a desert island, I felt totally isolated, without knowing how to swim. My world was entirely different from the world of my friends with normal children. Their concerns, questions and joy about their child raising had no connection to me. How could I sympathize with my friend who complained that her eighteen-month-old was into everything, when all my eighteen-month-old did was sit like a Buddha, rocking back and forth, in quiet contemplation of his hands or of his family around him? I no longer shared a common language with my friends.

One of my greatest tasks, then, in dealing with my two special children, has been to build a bridge from my "island" to the mainland inhabited by my friends. It began as a very unsteady, rough, irregular crossing. It was especially difficult, because there was no known cause or diagnosis for my children's developmental delays. Not only were the professionals confused, so was I. It was the worst time for me – the beginning of all my questioning. I was left wide open for examination and instruction from those around me. What might be a simple suggestion to parents of normally progressing children, took on much more significance for me.

If a friend says to a mother whose child is developing normally, "You are not giving that child enough stimulating activities," the mother can look at her child and see that he is growing and thriving and doing just fine. She can respond to her friends accordingly. When someone says that to me, it is not so easy to shrug off. My child is not growing and thriving normally. Even if I feel he is getting all the stimulation he can handle, my friend does not believe I know what I am talking about.

In those early days, I was often blamed by well-meaning friends as the cause behind my children's delay. And if I weren't the cause, I was a hindrance to their normal development.

Many friends told me I worried too much. I was overprotective. Where was my trust in a higher wisdom? I was given a tremendous amount of advice about how to change my outlook as well as my parenting skills. I became the focus.

Gradually, as people realized there was something different about Benjamin and Naomi, above and beyond the normal, the focus began to change from me to them. My children became a challenge – a puzzle to be solved. Various friends told me what exercises would be good for them, what doctors they should see, what medications they should take, and in what activities they should engage.

I was also told of all the things I must not do. Needless to say, the advice was conflicting. I did as much as I could for my children, but constantly felt guilty that I was not doing enough.

Many people had no idea that what they read in a book or heard in a lecture regarding children, was often not appropriate when applied to different real life situations. Nor do I think they were aware how all of their advice lacked thoughtful human outreach and support.

Many of my friends are involved in growing and changing, searching and seeking. Most of my friends are well read. Strangely enough, it was often preconceived knowledge that got in the way of my friends being helpful. I wonder how often the thoughts we learn in school, read in books, and listen to in lectures, come between our truly seeing the situation or human being before us. We are so easily drawn into applying our knowledge, expanding our knowledge, and putting our hard-earned knowledge to use that we forget to set it aside for just a moment to observe each person, each new situation afresh. I am always amazed at the openness and wonder of life my daughter has. We could all use more of that wonder and ability to see things anew.

People often tell me that they could not do what I do as the mother of Naomi and Benjamin. These are my children. I love them. I don't have one friend who couldn't handle parenting a child with special needs. They might not want to, but they could, and they would if faced with the challenge.

I also have some friends who feel the need to remind me that my life could be much worse. Some of these same friends refuse to relate to anything in my life as being out of the ordinary. For example, one friend complained to me that her little toddler Benjamin's age was talking all the time, and what should she do. My Benjamin is still at the non-specific babbling stage. Although she knew perfectly well that he was not talking, I reminded her again. She responded that Benjamin would soon be talking and that I would wish he were quiet. My friend added that she had just seen a movie about a child who couldn't speak or hear, and that I should be grateful Benjamin is not like that.

I never really know what to say to these people. I usually just try to avoid them. For some reason their comments always hurt. They make me feel more alone and misunderstood than ever.

I do not wallow in grief that my life is different than I planned. Nor do I deny it. Some of my best friends have normal children. We share some of the same and some different parenting experiences, and can still be close. All I ask of my friends is that they accept my children for who they are. No more. No less. A child must not be denied his or her unique individuality.

Of course, my situation could be worse. No matter how bad things are, they could always be worse. They could also be better. What bearing does that have on reality? It is the way it is, and that is what I have to work with. From that place I must begin. I can reflect on many "what ifs". Eventually, I must begin to work with what is. Only then can I grow.

I know that it is not always easy to find the right thing to say to the parent of a child with special needs. Thirteen years ago my brother had a daughter who was born blind. I said all the wrong things. I felt I was being very supportive. I could feel my brother, with whom I had been very close, drifting farther and farther away. We were in two different worlds. I had a wonderful relationship with his daughter. She was precious. Although she was blind, I thought my brother could surely see what a special little human being she was. I knew her blindness was a shock, but soon, I thought, he would learn to accept her disability.

I think that is what most of my friends thought about my children, too. They did not realize that there is much more to acceptance than that.

Parents of children with special needs are struggling to accept and to cope with a whole new direction in life, filled with immense responsibilities for which our society offers no training, little understanding and even less support.

Most of us can understand a parent accepting her special child. However, our understanding often ends there. The parent is becoming a very different person and we don't understand. Feelings of anger, jealousy, insecurity or rejection can emerge in us. The parent is re-evaluating, re-defining, and re-examining her life. We fit into her life differently now. She has changed; she is growing. She has no choice. A friend or relative can grow too. The choice is theirs.

I found that in the friends or relatives who gave me the most support, what they said or didn't say was not as relevant as their inner state of being. They trusted in me as a human being, and accepted that I was becoming a different person. If I needed to complain, however irrational, they just listened and had confidence that when I could, I would be rational again. Never did they advise me how to raise my children. What they gave me was acceptance, respect and a great amount of love.

I have added some very valuable friends as a result of parenting my two children. These friends are also parents of children with disabilities. Although our children's handicaps are different, we share a common understanding, which only comes from parenting a disabled child.

As I learn how to get around my little island, I feel much more comfortable on the mainland with the rest of the world. Some friends I do not see very often any more. Others are trying, each in his or her own way, to help bridge a common bridge between us. For that I am grateful.

JENNI:

After the birth of our children, when many friends just seemed to melt away, I learned that if I reach out towards others, others generally will come towards me. Of course I have sometimes felt very alone; of course I have known some rebuffs. Yet through it all, I have found that many people, both close friends and distant acquaintances, were waiting for a sign from me to tell them that I wanted to talk. Though not every relationship has been as supportive as the few deep friendships have been, still, communication lines have remained open. Early on,

I had to take the conscious step to pick up the telephone and make arrangements to see people. Sometimes this meant inviting someone for a cup of tea, even though I could scarcely spare the time, and the house was a mess. But I felt then, and still do, that investing time in friendships is more important than doing housework or ironing. Often we get together with other families on Sunday afternoons. We generally go out for a long walk, then share a simple supper of bread and cheese. From time to time I have arranged to spend time alone with an individual friend, so we could really talk and share (not always about children, either). And sometimes we invite a whole bunch of friends over at once for a party. The important thing has been to take the initiative, to go out towards people.

I also believe that in order to have friends one has to *be* a friend. This means not talking about one's own problems all the time, nor imposing one's emotions on others, though of course we all share feelings from time to time. There are counsellors and trained therapists whose job it is specifically to listen to our problems and help us release our emotions. Friends are for laughing with, sharing experiences with, giving and taking. Maybe one's friend has a problem too. Doing little gestures – giving a lift home from a meeting, treating to a cup of coffee, taking back a library book – go a long way in feeding a friendship, and showing others that despite our own troubles, we recognise and care for them, too.

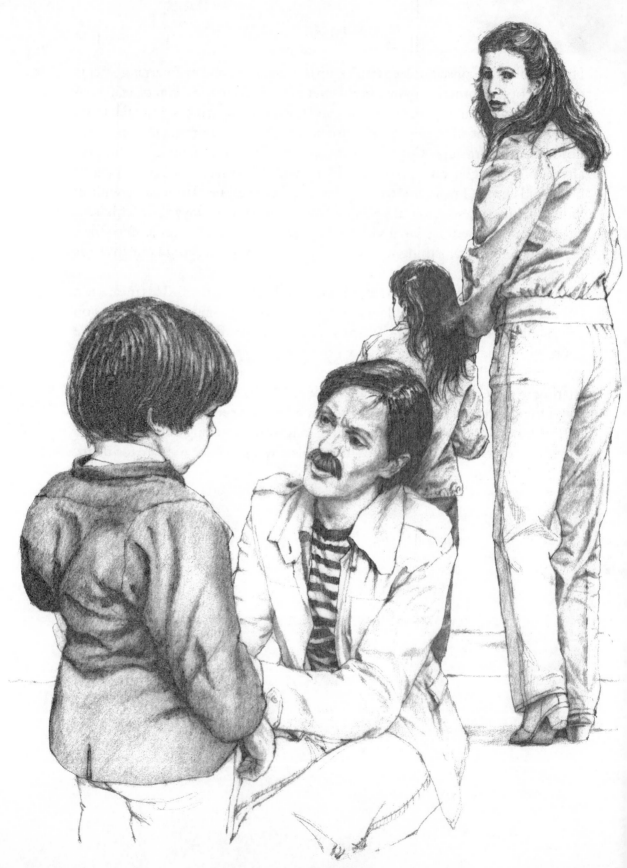

Attitudes

# 9

## *Attitudes*

*"… and yet, the spastic baby would ever be the soul which would never kill, maim, creed falsehood or hate brotherhood. Why then does society fear the crippled child, wondered Joseph out loud, and why does it hail the able-bodied child and crow over what may in time become a potential executioner?."*

Christopher Nolan
*Under the Eye of the Clock,* 1988

PADDY:

Throughout their lives the parents of handicapped children will find within themselves a variety of emotions. Additionally they will often find themselves short of sleep and physically exhausted which makes the daily routine even harder, to which can be added frustration at events and officialdom. Naturally not all react in the same way – some may feel unable to cope or others excessively anxious or bowed down, while many are carried along by deep enduring love for their offspring. Tides of different emotions will come and go, all will experience frustration many times.

The important thing is to discard or find a release for negative feelings. You will want to channel and conserve energies so that nothing destroys you as parents, or your relationship with your child and the rest of the family. It helps to be cheerful and positive. It is natural to ask Why? but pointless to labour the question too long, for it only adds to the existing problems. Far better to accept, make decisions, learn as you go along. Try to relax, appreciate the joyful for there is much if you seek it, avoid comparisons, emphasize the good, deal with the bad then forget it.

In the early stages of a child's growth some professionals became obsessed with conventional milestones. In most cases these are not the same for the handicapped person as for others as their steps forward are smaller and slower, each going at their own pace. Progress though slight is there so parents should watch for and appreciate each little improvement. Ignore all the 'He should be doing.....' 'Why doesn't she....' Set aside each day a short time to learn together and love each other. One of the great advantages of the programmes especially devised for the handicapped – or even sound alternative therapies, be they music or foot massage, is that the child is getting a great deal of individual attention born of love for that youngster and everyone thrives on affection.

It is wise to take into consideration too, the attitude of others – often thoughtless and unkind, occasionally even cruel, much of it born of embarrassment and not knowing 'the right thing to say'. It all serves to highlight the loving, caring approaches which can nevertheless be found surprisingly often. Unfortunately, the 'experts' in medicine, education, and welfare are often the ones who project negative attitudes and contribute to the unhappiness of parents. This is why the parents of special children need to find internal and external courage to trust their own judgment, to value themselves for they know their child better than anyone else and to seek advice all the time but weigh it for appropriateness. Learn to stand back calmly and view your child in perspective.

The learning process in the handicapped will be slow but they can learn, they will progress, they do mature. They love to learn both with Mother and Pa and when the time comes, to go to school like all the others. Sam, though only functioning at perhaps four or five years, has nevertheless matured slowly and (with one exception) has adored her schools and teachers. She is still fearful about noise, machinery, thunderstorms and new experiences but has learned to say she's frightened, come for comfort whilst at other times she reverts to biting her wrist or a good old-fashioned tantrum. I wait for this to stop, as it does eventually, then we talk about the problem, have lots of hugs and reassurance and know this is a step towards coping with what are to her the frightening aspects of life, one most dreadful part being her inability to fully articulate her fears.

HELEN:

Always one of the things we come face-to-face with when we are with Keziah is our own inadequacies. Imagine: *we* get angry and frustrated at Keziah's spasticity, her inability to sit down, her imperfect head control, etc. What is it like for her? To be inside a body that will not do anything you ask it to and try to do. Keziah invariably meets our anger with benevolent smiles which, in the heat of the moment, leaves one more angry or guilty. Later, when we reflect, we can only wonder at the greatness of her soul. Spiritually she has greater strength and capability than the two of us combined. We have so much to learn from her and children like her. Such thoughts come in serene moments and more rarely in the thick of things when we are trying to feed a spitting, dribbling Keziah.

We believe Keziah has come to us for a purpose, which we *all* have chosen. We also share a faith that this is right. It is what we all need, although sometimes our small selves reject the handicap as a mistake, as 'wrong' and say "no" and "Why us?" This faith, combined with love for each other, brings us through the rough patches and gives us contentment in the good phases.

With faith in the rightness of things, comes an attitude of service towards Keziah. She leads the way, shining forth, and encouraging us to follow. All we need to do for her, and all we want to do for her, is an act of service, an offering, for this great soul who has chosen such a difficult task. Keziah gives us all a chance to give freely, and to face our own imperfections in so doing. Do I want to know how selfish I can be? Or how impatient or bad tempered? Having said that, I think we must learn too to be kind to ourselves… always allow ourselves space to do better but also not to feel guilty or a failure when we do not meet our own standards. Parenting of any child is a lot about seeing who you are and what you are.

HOLLY:

These children have pulled out of me a strength and depth and determination I did not know I had. I guess no one ever demanded such things from me as my children have.

I certainly haven't always been grateful for all that they have so innocently expected from me. I have felt sorry for myself, angry at God, guilt that I did something wrong, doubt that I was doing anything right, fear of what was so unknown, lonely because all my friends had normal children, and misunderstood because no one really knows what it is like to be a parent of a handicapped child.

None of these feelings were directed at my childen. Rather, they were directed at my own relationship to life. Suddenly, there was so much I didn't know. So much over which I had no control. So little help from others. Not because they didn't want to help, but because they didn't know how to help. And I didn't know how to help them.

My life became very different from what I had always envisioned. Although I spent several years living and working with all kinds of handicapped children, being a parent to a child with special needs is a totally different experience.

So here I am: My daughter is five. My son is two. I am one-hundred and thirty, and I still have much to learn. My children haven't even reached adolescence!

I still have days when I am overwhelmed by grief, when I am angry at the world, and when I am sorry for myself. I would like to experience more inner peace, more equanimity, and more trust in the spiritual world. I am working on these goals.

I have excellent teachers. My children have helped me to grow in areas I did not know were lacking. They have given me the opportunity to put aside all my expectations of how children ought to be: how they should behave or how much they should accomplish.

I have had to really look at my children, study them, feel them – feel what it must be like to be Benjamin or Naomi. To rid myself of as much subjective reaction as possible, and to replace it with objectivity. I did not realise before what a difficult task this is. So much is deeply embedded in our very core which must be set aside. Yet, when I am able to overcome my subjectivity, I am aware of yet another gift that my children have given me.

This gift is a very special kind of love that permeates my whole being and embraces all I see. It needs nothing in return. My children need not perform or live up to any preconceived notions of what a child ought to be. It is not the everyday love I have for my children. It is a love that washes over me at a moment's notice, leaving in its place a renewed strength and gratefulness for the many wonderful blessings I have in life.

The love I have grows out of truly seeking, observing, studying, contemplating, and finally finding the highest and truest individuality in my two children. Everyone has a unique and individual personality, but I have learned that there is something even deeper, or should I say higher, which lies at the very core of every human being.

At two and one-half, my little Benjamin has a favourite game. He can spend an hour at a time all by himself in studious contemplation of a small block. He first places the block on the coffee table. He then sits back, studies it from various angles, knocks it off, listens for the sound it makes, observes whether his mighty throw propelled it far or near, to the left or to the right. He then crawls over to it, picks it up, turns it over in his hands, touching and looking at every corner. Back to the coffee table he brings it, repeating his entire experiment, all the while stopping to study it at each step.

When Benjamin tires of the coffee table, Benjamin tries his block experiment on the bookcase. Later, he tests balancing it on the top of a ball, or perhaps a pillow. He does this experiment with all kinds of items – a string, a marble, a leaf, a stone. If I am there watching him, he turns, laughs and smiles to me, wiggling his hands and feet, expressing with his whole body how excited he is to make such incredible discoveries. He then returns to his experiments, continuing to learn more about the world around him.

The neurologist tells me that Benjamin is functioning at a significantly retarded level. Yes, he certainly is far behind his peers in outwardly observable abilities. Yet, when I watch Benjamin as he plays, I see a being inside my son that is absolutely perfect. That is the part of Benjamin that cannot be improved upon. That is the part that tells me who Benjamin really is. That is the part I strive to ever hold in my heart. This perfect being which lives in my children is what I always try to keep in my consciousness. Although it often disappears, in the most trying and not-so-trying moments, I find that when I am able to stop for a moment to regain that clearer, truer picture, I gain the strength to meet my children where they are.

## PADDY:

Let us pay homage to the importance of love in the life of a handicapped person for they profit both from receiving and giving love. It is the power which motivates and strengthens parents to care for and go on caring for their handicapped youngster in the face of enormous pressures and problems and it gets them through the heartaches, hard work and hassles met every day. It generates that spirit which bonds together the families of the handicapped so that they form a protective, encouraging environment.

Most teachers of handicapped people love their charges too, so we should not overlook its purpose in their lives also. Therefore, do not be afraid or embarrassed about loving your handicapped person. Be proud of their small achievements and let them know it. Encourage pride in their natures too for the efforts necessary in their lives are often much greater than for us lesser mortals – so love them and stand tall and teach them to love themselves and appreciate their own worth.

Additionally, help them to show affection and love to those around them and in contact with them. Perhaps it is too easy for handicapped youngsters to be and appear to be selfish if we do everything for them. Saying 'I'm glad *you* love me!' or '*Your* lovely smile cheers me up so much' avows their worth to others. Parents can be a little diffident about declaring their love for their handicapped offspring almost as though we shouldn't be seen to love one who is not perfect – What nonsense. Happiness, joy, love can come from so many sources. Hug your child often.

Infancy

# 10

# Infancy

JENNI:

All new-born babies need to be loved, held and cuddled – regardless of their shape, size, limb formation or disability. They have been formed in the wholeness of the womb, and each young personality will develop more wholesomely if we give complete affection, regardless of any well-founded worries about the future. Sometimes they need "special care" and technical intervention. Then we must reassure them that it won't be for ever, and let that affection be so strong and caring that it seeps through the glass side of the incubator!

Even "normal" babies do not have fully developed sight and hearing at birth. They respond to touch, to being handled, fed and spoken to. They need sleep and peace for the gradual awakening that is growth.

If your baby has an obvious sight or hearing deficiency that is already known just after birth, you will want to relate with particular consideration to your infant's beginning awareness. Peggy Freeman, herself the mother of a deaf/blind child, gives this picture:

*"For instance your baby is nice and warm and cosy in his cot and he sees and hears nothing to warn him that you have come to the cot and are about to pick him up say to give him a bath – out of the blue a pair of hands take him up in the air, put him down again in a place that is not his cosy cot, his clothes are taken off, he is lifted again and put in yet another strange environment – imagine this had happened to you and then on top of it all a wet soapy hand you had not seen coming slides over your body – quite enough to upset you (and your appetite) for the rest of day! Even when you got used to the idea that this would happen frequently, you would still be likely to feel fear."[1]*

She suggests ways of communicating with baby:
*"At all times before you go to pick up your baby from the cot or pram, lay your hand*

*very gently on him and leave it there for a few seconds – this is to become the signal that*
*something is going to happen to him. If he is in a cot with a drop side, give him this signal*
*before you let the side down and do let it down gently. Lift him slowly and firmly from the*
*cot and make the place in your lap as cosy as the bed he has just left. Take your time*
*undressing or changing him – baby clothes that slip on and off easily without him having to*
*be moved about too much help to make it easy for you both. When it is bathtime have the*
*room warm and the towel warmed. Try to have the bath the same height as your lap so*
*that baby does not have the feeling of a drop as he goes into it. Your warning signal for this*
*part of the routine could be just to dabble baby's hand in the warm water before actually*
*immersing his body. Be careful about the heat of the bath – if your baby has a heart defect*
*his feet and hands may be extra cold and what seems to you to be a suitable temperature for*
*his body may actually feel burning to his toes and fingers. An experience of this kind can*
*make bathing something to be feared for a very long time which is a pity, because*
*deaf/blind children get a lot of pleasure from the feel of water as well as useful limb*
*movement. If your baby's feet and hands feel cold before the bath, warm them gently until*
*they are the same temperature as the rest of his body, do not make the water cooler."*[2]

Bath-time can be enjoyable for many babies with special needs  –  tiny limbs
which cannot kick properly will become weightless and graceful in the water,
touch and trust can build up confidence and general well-being.

If you can manage breast-feeding, this is a tremendous asset. (See "Food and
Feeding".)

You will want to consider the logistics of nappy changing, dressing, bathing,
and laundry to make everything as practical and convenient as possible. In one
flat where we lived, we built a changing table at waist height over the bathtub,
which could lift up on hinges when a big person wanted to take a bath. Ask your
social worker about possible grants for some improvements like this if money
and resources are short.

We found that our children generally needed medical attention sooner than
other babies did, to prevent a casual illness turning into a major one. Follow
your intuition if breathing doesn't sound right, or a cough is too persistent, and
seek advice.

*If you have cause for concern and cannot reach the doctor, go direct to the hospital*
*casualty or emergency section for immediate attention.*

You may wish to keep a book on your baby, containing notes made at regular
intervals, photos, dates, special cards, and records of major events. If it is painful

to try to fill in a standard "baby book" with printed pictures of cute babies or fluffy animals, then try an unlined drawing book from a shop which sells artists' supplies. This way you write what you want, rather than having to conform to the usual infant milestones. I try to include photos, which over time have been a great help in noticing subtle changes in the children which escaped my observation in daily life. The books have also been invaluable when we have taken the children to see new consultants, or to meet a new teacher at school.

We have asked each doctor we consulted to give us copies of letters, results of tests, and resumés of hospitalisations. These are kept in a file, along with a record of all illnesses with medications given, dates of vaccinations, growth and weight charts (a doctor or health visitor should be able to supply these), and a list with dates of all X-rays, dental check-ups, eye and ear check-ups. In addition we have a blood-type certificate for each child which we requested the first time each child had a blood test. We were also able to obtain a photocopy of each birth record, which included details of the labour, the baby's height, weight and head circumference and Apgar scores. As parents, *we are our children's most powerful advocates*. Having a file with all these records has not only helped us to talk with doctors and other health-care professionals, but it has also enabled us to see relationships between events, and spot problems before they go too far. We have our children's best interests at heart, and being able to prove a point using the relevant medical record has helped us several times to get better treatment for our children.

Our daughter, like so many children with handicaps, spent a large part of her infancy in hospital. After this experience I feel it is utterly important to fight to stay with one's child, to tell her what is happening or going to happen, and be with her through any tests or painful treatment. I know this is not so simple in many hospitals where the policy seems to view parent participation as a nuisance, or worse. (To be fair, these attitudes do seem to be changing for the better in recent years.) As parents, it is important, then, that we pick only *big* battles to fight, and learn to distinguish between the essentials (the emotional and physical well-being of the child), and non-essentials (diet, clothing, routines, ways of doing things). We also need to be sensitive to the workload of medical staff, their long hours and stress symptoms, not to cause unnecessary conflict. At the same time we should remember that this is, after all, *our* child, and we have the moral right (if not always the "right" in the hospital rulebook) to accompany, comfort and advocate for her.

Finally, I find it very important to *let go* of infancy when the time comes. For me, letting go has meant allowing other people to care for my child, dressing her more maturely, changing toys, activities, and room decorations and, most difficult, changing my own inner picture of her. In a way I feel this is most important when the child remains at the infant level developmentally; then having an inner picture of her as being her real chronological age helps me not to "baby" her, but rather to look for the full richness of which she is really capable.

1. and 2. *Understanding the Deaf/Blind Child* by Peggy Freeman (Heinemann Health Books, London 1975). pp 4 and 5.

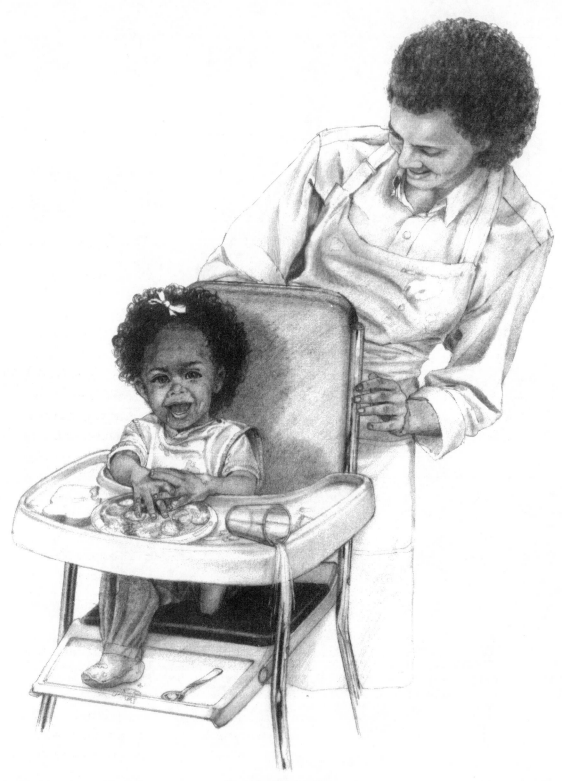

Food and feeding

# 11

## *Food and Feeding*

JENNI:

If you read this in the early days after your baby's birth, please consider breast feeding. For a child born with a handicap, it can be a vital factor in early development. It is well known today that breast milk is *the* perfect infant food, provides protective anti-bodies, helps prevent allergies and fosters early mother-infant bonding. For a baby with a handicap, any one of the above advantages would be enough to warrant breast feeding. There are many other advantages as well, which are less well known. For instance, a child born with a sensory handicap will learn to orient himself earlier, and with more confidence if he has enjoyed a secure breast feeding relationship; a baby with cerebral palsy will be helped towards normal eating skills (swallowing, sucking, normal tongue control) if she has had the opportunity to suck normally at the breast; a child with autism can often gain immeasurable comfort through breast feeding, sometimes the only physical contact that such a child can endure in the early months; a premature or low-birthweight baby grows best when fed his mother's milk, the one food which his immature digestive system can cope with, and which is tailor-made for his specific needs; a child who must undergo early surgery has heightened chances for good recovery when she can feel secure in the nursing relationship; and babies born with metabolic disorders such as diabetes, hypoglycemia and phenylketonurea (PKU) may gain extra benefit from breast milk in conjunction with highly-specialized infant formulas they may need.[1]

For mothers, too, the breast feeding relationship can bring many rewards: the shock and grief of having a baby born with a handicap can be significantly healed through the close contact of feeding the baby at the breast; for mothers whose babies are in an incubator or on life-support systems, providing breast milk for their child may be the one act they feel they can *do* for the child, who is otherwise taken out of their care; and the bond created through breastfeeding in the early months can help a mother understand her child's needs in an intuitive way. This can help in moments of medical emergency, and also in daily life when the child is trying to communicate his needs but has no language to express himself. Breast feeding is so normal, mothers have done it down through the ages. Sharing such an ancient and timeless act can bring a welcome sense of normality to a relationship which has otherwise been invaded by technology, stress, grief, and separation.

I breast-fed all of my children, and I know from experience how difficult it can be! My first child suffered from a cleft palate, had a mental handicap which destroyed the sucking reflex and the hunger reflex, and caught a salmonella diarrhoea while in Intensive Care and lost nearly a third of her birth weight through severe dehydration.

My second child also had a cleft palate. My third child had neither the normal sucking reflex, nor the hunger reflex, due to the unspecified condition which has caused his subsequent developmental delay. I pumped my breast-milk for over 18 months. I re-established my milk supply which had vanished during an early separation from my first child. I joined a breast-feeding support group and eventually became a breast-feeding counsellor, to help other mothers who face similar problems as those I had to overcome. So from this standpoint, I would like to offer the following advice:

*Breast-feeding is a mother's and baby's right.* It is worth fighting for. Feeling militant about it can help you overcome the objections of doctors, nurses, unconvinced family members and badly-informed Health Visitors. Even if your child only receives *some* breastmilk *some* is infinitely *better than none.* If you want to breast-feed your child, don't let anybody say you can't!

*Monitor your baby's weight-gain carefully.* Slow weight-gain is one of the most common reasons for introducing artificial feeding, and with good reason. Babies with physical handicaps often have problems sucking hard enough to get enough milk for proper growth. Babies with mental or neurological handicaps may experience no hunger, have no sucking reflex. and need to be awakened and "forced" to feed. Premature babies may be too weak to suck, yet need to gain weight urgently to survive. So I would advise you to weigh your baby every day with no clothes on, before the same feed of the day, until the birth-weight has been regained. Then I would advise weighing the child every few days until a good weight-gain curve has been charted, (ask your Doctor or Health Visitor to give you appropriate charts) then weighing every week or two throughout the first six months of life. If your child does not gain regularly, maintaining at least the minimum acceptable weight-gain curve, then you will need to take swift action to ensure that your baby gets more to eat. Some ways to do this are: increasing the frequency of feeds, (an infant who is totally breastfed may take up to 10 or 12 feeds per 24 hours), giving both breasts at least twice during every feed, (this stimulates milk production and makes sure the child gets full benefit of the richer "hind" milk), and topping up with infant formula if absolutely necessary.

*Stimulating your milk supply:* the Golden Rule here is supply and demand: the more milk the baby takes, the more milk will be produced. *Do* give more frequent feeds, *do* give each breast at least twice during each feed, *do* drink at least a full glass of liquid before or during each feed, *do* empty both breasts (either manually or with a breast pump) after each feed, collecting the extra milk in sterile bottles to "top up" later feeds as needed, and *do* make sure you are eating a hearty, well-balanced diet. On the other hand, *don't* skip a feed (you won't have more milk the next time, but less), *don't* try to diet, smoke a lot, rush around all day long, and *don't* listen if anyone says to you: "Your milk is too thin," "You're too tired, Dear, why don't you give the baby a bottle?" "You'll never have enough milk," "You'll never manage to get your milk supply back," "Breast-feeding will ruin your breasts," or "Are you trying to starve your baby?" (These were all actual comments that I received during my months of breastfeeding.)

*Re-establishing your milk supply:*[2] It is possible to completely re-establish your milk supply, even days or weeks after last feeding your baby. As long as you can express just *one drop* of milk, you *can* build up a full supply again. To do this you will need perseverance. You will also need to monitor your baby's weight closely, because the transition from formula to breast-milk must be carried out carefully so that the baby always gets what he needs. Re-establishing a milk supply is based on two principles: *lots of stimulation* for milk production, and *gradual elimination* of formula. If your baby is able to suck directly at the breast, the first thing to do is to put the baby to the breast, giving each breast *at least twice, before* each bottle feed. At the same time, it helps to give extra feeds at the breast between the bottle feeds, to give extra stimulation. The frequency will naturally diminish as the baby grows and is able to suck harder at each feed, and go longer between feeds. You should feel a significant increase in milk production within 24 hours, though this may not yet be enough to meet all the baby's needs. Carry on, and already by the third and fourth days you should have quite a lot of milk on hand. At the same time, starting on the first day, or as soon as you feel your milk begin to let down a little bit, begin to reduce the amount of formula you are giving in each bottle, say by half an ounce or an ounce, per bottle. Obviously if the baby is completely satisfied by the formula, he won't be as interested in sucking to stimulate your milk supply. On the other hand, his needs *must* be met at all times, because being a "baby at risk", there is less leeway, and weight loss can be that much more dangerous. But if the baby seems satisfied after a breast-feed, don't feel you have to give the whole bottle. Take your cue from your baby. Beware, however, of the baby who does not wake for feeds. Such a baby can actually be losing weight, but due to his neurological handicap, does not experience hunger, I would advise never to let a newborn, or an infant with problems gaining weight, sleep more than 4 hours at a stretch. You may need to remind him how hungry he really is! If the baby's daily weight-gain is satisfactory during the time you are re-establishing your milk supply, then by all means continue reducing the amount of formula given when he appears satisfied.

If your baby can feed at the breast but has a weak suck, you may find that the baby's sucking is not enough to re-establish or augment your milk supply. Perhaps your baby sucks just long enough to make your milk let down, but not enough to empty the breast. Then you are left with milk in your breasts. This will gradually reduce your milk supply, because your breasts are not being emptied, *even though the baby needs all the milk that is being produced*. In either of these cases, you will probably find an electric breast pump essential. With the pump you can completely empty your breasts after each feed, storing the milk in sterile bottles in the fridge, to top up the baby's *next* feed. (Don't try to pump your milk for a screaming baby, it's just too stressful!) To empty your breasts completely using the electric pump you will need to switch back and forth between your breasts several times the way you would with the baby at the breast. Not only does this stimulate the milk production, but it significantly increases the amount of milk you will get, because it is possible to experience two let-downs during a feed, and switching back and forth will fully empty the milk from the second let-down. If you have fed the baby, say, an hour ago, and pumped your milk afterwards, you may feel you have nothing in your breasts to offer your child if he wakes again. Don't worry, *milk is being produced all the time,* and it is worth putting the baby back to the breast and switching back and forth between breasts a few times *before* you top up either with expressed milk or formula.

Having had two children with cleft palates, I am well aware that some babies just simply cannot feed at the breast, or if they do, they cannot manage to suck hard enough to get any milk. The more frustrated and hungry the baby gets, the more difficult it is to get him to nurse. You can offset this problem with the "supplemental infant feeder". In the U.K. it is called the Axicare Nursing Aid, and is sold by Colgate Medical Ltd., 1 Fairacres Estate, Dedworth Road, Windsor, Berks. SL4 4LE telephone (0753) 860378. In the U.S. it is called the Lact-Aid, and is sold by the Division of Resources in Human Nurturing, Box 6861, Denver, CO 80206. This device consists of a plastic bag to contain expressed breast-milk (or formula) which is hung from the mother's neck, between her breasts. A plastic tube leads from the milk-bag to the mother's nipple. As the infant sucks the nipple, he also receives milk from the tube. The mother's milk-supply is stimulated by the sucking and closeness with the baby, and the baby gets the benefit of feeding at the breast without the danger of not getting enough to eat. As a simpler version of the same principle, I have read in La Leche League literature of mothers who have filled a sterilized, (unused!) plastic hair-dye bottle bought empty at the chemist's. While the baby sucks at the breast, supplemental milk is fed into the corner of the baby's mouth through the pointed tube on the bottle. Some babies are in intensive care or are simply too weak or fragile to suck at the breast, yet could benefit immensely from feeding "at the breast" once they have gained enough strength.

*Pumping Breast-milk:* When we brought our daughter home from the hospital, I had to re-establish my milk supply without the benefit of her sucking directly at the breast, because she could not suck at all. I pumped my milk regularly, at the same times every day, including during the night in the beginning. In all, I pumped my milk five times a day, (a minimum frequency, I would think). I took about half an hour each time, switching back and forth between my breasts about 10 or 15 times during each pumping session. I massaged my breasts before I started with herbal oil, (made by Weleda, and containing aromatic essences of fennel, caraway and anis, which are thought to be milk-stimulating). I think any nice-smelling vegetable oil, (especially almond oil, or wheat germ oil, which is rich in vitamin E and helps prevent cracked nipples) would be helpful. I massaged each breast as I pumped it, from the outside towards the area just around the nipple. This brings the milk down from where it is produced, to the reservoirs behind the areola, where it is stored until the baby (or milk pump) extracts it from the breast. Massaging helps increase the milk flow enormously, and, by making sure all areas of the breast are massaged equally, it also helps to empty the breast completely.

While I pumped my milk I used to drink a pint of milk, non-alcoholic beer, or fruit juice, to make sure I got enough fluids. I also would prop up a good book against the side of the pump. This helped pass the time, and gave me the feeling that *I* was also getting something out of the exercise! The electric pump we rented made a loud, droning noise, not unlike the base note of a bag-pipe. My husband used to sing Breton and Celtic songs to it, pretending it *was* a bag-pipe! A little humour sure goes a long way!

I also found it helped to take vitamins, (a multi-B complex, E and cod liver oil tablets for A and D). This kept me from getting too run down from all the fatigue and stress. If I happened to forget to take them one morning, I could feel the difference by noon. Eating a high-protein breakfast helped me with extra energy throughout the day. The long-lasting energy of the protein seemed to help me tackle the day's problems more easily.

If you feel that an electric breast pump would be useful to you, you can rent one by contacting your local National Childbirth Trust breast-feeding counsel-lor, or the nearest branch of the La Leche League. Though renting the pump will cost money, it works out to be less than the cost of buying infant formula. At the time of writing, the current rental prices in Britain are 55p/day if you have a baby with a handicap, cleft palate or who is premature. If you are in financial difficulty due to unemployment, or if you receive Supplementary Benefit, the rental fee can be reduced to 22p/day. If you still cannot afford to pay, it is worth asking your social worker to help you find a charity or fund who could help with the cost. If you have no local NCT group, you can also contact the pump manufacturer directly:

U.K.: Ameda-Egnell Breast Pump, Unit 2, Belvedere Trading Estate, Taunton, Somerset, TA1 1BH. Telephone: (0823) 336362

U.S.A.: Ameda-Egnell Breast Pump, 765 Industrial Drive, Carey, IL 60013. Telephone (312) 639-2900

*Storing Breast Milk:* As it comes from the breast, milk will always be sterile (barring acute breast infection). However, if you need to give it to your baby by bottle it is important to be as hygienic as possible. This means sterilizing all bottles, pump equipment and teats between each use, as well as washing hands and breasts with mild soap before each time you pump your milk. Breast-milk which is stored in sterile bottles can be kept for a day in the refrigerator. You should take a fresh bottle each time you pump your milk, and let it cool down in the refrigerator before adding it to the rest of the milk stored that day. This is because adding warm milk to cold milk can make it go off. If your baby doesn't finish a bottle, don't "keep it for next time," because the germs in his saliva can also quickly make milk turn. If you think you will need to keep freshly-pumped milk for more than a day, it is better to collect it, as outlined above, then freeze it in the quantities you will need for each feed. Frozen milk can be thawed by putting the bottle in warm, not hot, water (to avoid cooking it). The NCT and La Leche League strongly discourage warming bottles of milk in the microwave oven.

*Introducing Solid Food:* The National Childbirth Trust and La Leche League, suggest introducing solids around six months of age. If your child's growth and weight gain has been within the normal limits, and he can suck and control his tongue normally, then introducing solids will be essentially the same as for any other baby. If your child's weight gain has been slow, or he was born prematurely, it might be wise to consult a breastfeeding counsellor, health visitor or doctor regarding the best time to begin solids. If weight is a serious problem, solids can be given to *supplement* the milk feeds, rather than to replace any of them. The question of when to wean the baby is a highly personal one, and I feel the mother should follow her own intuition, regardless of the advice she may receive from many different sides. A baby who has been separated from her mother, undergone painful medical treatment or operations, or has not benefitted from the full amount of home care and cuddling, may well need longer breastfeeding, (or bottle feeding, held in the mother's arms) to offset the earlier emotional stress. At some point, it will also be an important step for the child to be weaned; when the baby has a handicap, letting go of the nursing relationship is just as crucial for both the baby and mother, as establishing the nursing relationship was in the first place. Often through infancy and childhood it will be the mother's task to help her child to separate from her, even though he cannot take the step that a "normal" child would at the same age. This process can be very painful for the mother, because letting go of babyhood when the child may be still at the baby stage developmentally, may emphasize all the differences. I found that taking up baby-food preparation with the same enthusiasm I gave breastfeeding, helped offset the feelings of ending the special feeding relationship. And for me, giving up the breast pump was a tremendous relief!

If you can, do buy one of those hand food grinders, (French moulis) that are sold in kitchenware shops. If you already have a blender or a food processor, these work well, too. Your initial financial investment will be repaid very quickly when compared to the cost of commercial baby food. When cooking for the rest of the family it is simple to take out a bit of food before you add salt or spices, and grind it up for the baby. When my children were little I cooked them a pot of mixed vegetables every morning and added a handful of organic five grain flakes, which boiled down very soft. Then I would purée or mash this as needed, adding some grated cheese or cottage cheese for protein. If we were having meat, I would purée this separately, as meat is sometimes harder to grind smoothly than vegetables. You may prefer to introduce meat much later, or not at all. Our easy, home-made desserts have included finely-grated raw fruit, stewed fruit, and plain yogurt or fromage frais, adding a bit of brown sugar if needed.

*Seating:* A child who lacks muscle control will need extra support while eating. For the child to swallow properly it is important that his head be at a normal angle, not thrown back, and that his torso is well supported. A reclining infant seat may work well in the early days, if the child is propped up well with pillows. Later on, your physiotherapist or occupational therapist will be able to advise you about special seats which have been designed with specific posture problems in mind (see section "How to Get Help").

It is equally important that the person feeding the child is comfortably seated, with the food within easy reach. A great deal of stress relating to feeding a child with a handicap arises because the feeder has to make repeated awkward movements, and cannot relax during feeding. It helps to have the child's entire meal ready on the table before starting. This avoids jumping up and down to get dishes, and is surely more peaceful for everyone.

*Feeding utensils:* There are many specially-designed utensils to help with feeding. Cutlery with easy-grip handles, tilted cups with wide handles on two sides, non-slip plates, and similar items can help children with motor handicaps gain independence in eating. As independence is the real goal, approach each step with the simplest solutions first, using normal utensils insofar as possible, opting for the specialized ones only when really necessary. Otherwise if your child becomes completely dependent on a particular item, say a special cup, and you happen to forget it one day while you are out visiting, your child may become very distraught. However, if he can cope with the normal range of utensils, perhaps with a bit of extra help if needed, then your whole family will be a lot freer to eat out or go away for a visit. When at home, and your child is coping without extra help, then specialized utensils can be a great boon.

## PADDY:

Lecturing on and discussing food and nutrition matters over the years has shown that this subject is the source of much worry and trouble. These seem to fall naturally into three groups:

1. What is good nutrition, particularly in relation to people with handicaps – that is, what should they and shouldn't they eat?
2. The problems that Mothers and the rest of the family encounter over various stages.
3. Useful hints to use and pass on.

Food can be a source of great pleasure to our youngsters from an early age but equally for others mealtimes can be distressing. Problems over food choice, eating habits, etc., can be a worry, particularly if for some reason it is felt the person's health or progress is adversely affected by how little or how much they eat or how fussy they are.

It is important to try to make mealtimes peaceful and relaxed occasions, bearing in mind that all children and youngsters seem to develop – early on – distinct likes and dislikes. Mothers easily and understandably become irritated by this, for standing over a hot stove then having your efforts rejected is galling. However, take comfort from stories about six foot, hefty, rugger playing types who – according to their ever-loving Mums – went through childhood on only mince, potatoes and ice-cream, never any vegetables, fruit or fibre. I know of one child who insisted on being vegetarian but didn't like vegetables!

Still, our youngsters do need nutritious foods including proteins (eggs, cheese, meat, pulses, fish and milk) grains, fresh fruit and vegetables. Fresh is stressed because the vitamin content is higher, they are crisper and thus more attractive to eat, and tinned fruit in particular is frequently (though less so now) packed in sugar syrup which is no help to teeth or slimness. Where small appetites are concerned or there are chewing difficulties, texture, appearance, and taste loom large. Life is easier all round if the parent can somehow accommodate the dislikes and fussing, understanding and accepting that new foods are most likely to be refused when introduced, and finding subtle ways to get nutritious foods accepted.

Because our youngsters often struggle with ill health and weight gain due to lack of exercise, 'junk foods' and empty calories must be avoided. Crisps, too much bread and pastry, sugar and sweets kill the appetite so that Johnnie doesn't want to eat now but is hungry later when all the stew has gone. They cause overweight, too.

From a few months old people recognise that parents become upset and perturbed at their refusal to eat and can use it as a weapon. Don't argue about eating, don't wheedle or nag because it won't help. Better to remove food, try later perhaps or give an alternative. I take the view that the Mother of a person with a handicap has to bend the rules in this situation because her youngster may not be able to explain what troubles him.

Using food as a 'bribe' is occasionally acceptable – like the odd packet of crisps, ice-cream or packet of allsorts but they should be kept for emergencies or reward. All parents need them so don't feel guilty.

Above all, though you may not understand why your child refuses certain foods or more perplexing why those once loved fall out of favour, just accept this. I strongly support the idea that people know when foods are not agreeing with them (particularly in the allergic sense) or the smell makes them feel sick, so *relax* and find other foods.

Equally, of course obsessions are just as worrying; the youngster will only eat or eats daily quantities of certain foods. My daughter, from age five, has adored bananas, once eating eighteen in one day and she still eats two or three most days now, for somehow they provide a missing but necessary substance for her metabolism. Many parents of handicapped youngsters report food obsessions (as they do obsessions with other things) that persist for many years. So how to handle this? Some eat and eat and eat and if you know they have a particular syndrome that requires food management then get what help exists from societies or dieticians. Be aware that in some cases when jam, sugar, ice-cream or chocolate are allowed this can trigger off a craving so it is probably better to avoid them altogether. It is advisable too, that the rest of the family eat sensibly and prevent the odd one out feeling victimised. Keep foods which you must deny right out of sight. Yes, other family members may suffer too, but everyone in the family must realise this is a difficult area with no easy answers and you are not the only people who have to battle this way.

One area of contention about foods is allergic reaction to certain ones and generally adverse results of eating others. Too many sweets, pastry, puddings and pies for instance cause spots, greasy hair, sallow skin – all unsightly and irritating. Worse still is that many youngsters seem to have problems with cow dairy products which can cause catarrh and sinusitis and the like. Others react badly to food colourings, in for instance fruit juices, jellies, canned goods. Replace cow's milk with goat or sheep milk and yogurt but understand that problems can take up to nine months or more to disappear, even longer, so don't expect instant results. Back your own hunch if your youngster seems to have problems which you suspect could be associated with certain foods (though some 'experts' will deny this). Excessive drowsiness, breathing problems, too many colds, even poor appetite may fit in here. Eggs, and wheat products can be a problem too, so if you are not sure or suspect certain foods withdraw them and keep a chart of exactly what is consumed – a bother but remarkably revealing. Dieticians know that anyone can be affected by any food at any time so don't ignore or dismiss any reaction. Read as much as possible on this subject for there are good books which make sensible suggestions. This aspect of the care of those handicaps is most important and my rule is… if they don't want to eat it don't make them.

*And now a few ideas which might help:* Seek out good quality bread of mixed grains when possible – rye or granary flour as well as wheat, for maximum benefit and flavour. If you eat meat, then liver is a good source of Vitamin B but most children hate it straight. Cooked lightly, then minced or liquidised then slipped into a stew or casserole it passes unnoticed. Liquidisers are invaluable for making meat, fish, vegetables into a more acceptable texture which slips down easily. Cabbage, sprouts, (actually any vegetable) liquidised then thinned with a little milk or cream or gravy is a good way of getting them in to the diet.

Colour is a governing factor in food acceptance or refusal more often than we think. Uninteresting foods like rice-pudding or stewed apples look more exciting with a tiny blob of jam in the middle; a few chopped nuts does the same.

Try eating out of unconventional dishes. Sam hates soup out of a cup but others may love it. Line a little basket with a paper napkin and put food in in small pieces for eating with their fingers. If food is fun it seems to be less of a problem. Another idea – a half slice of buttered bread, crustless, can be baked till crisp in bun tins then filled with stew, casserole, cauliflower cheese and the container eaten too!

Some problems over food are caused by eating difficulties so make things into small bite-sized pieces before offering. An apple in slivers can be coped with where quarters would be impossible.

*Finally some points to think about:* 'Special' people need three good meals a day and breakfast is *important* to start off the day for most travel distances to school or centre. If appetites are small five or six nutritious snacks in the day might be better than a big meal. Much bad temper and irritation is the result of being hungry or meals with too much sugar or starchy things and too low in protein. Don't offer choc bars or sweets if the youngster appears to need food – an apple or banana, wedge of cheese with carrot or celery stick is more sensible. Winter with its attendant coughs, colds, chest infections is unfortunately the time when stodgy food seems comforting but really only adds to the problems. Winter salads like coleslaw and waldorf are better than pastry, stewed fruit with perhaps a little yogurt or cream preferable to treacle tart. And lastly, do avoid sugar, it damages teeth and I believe increases hyper-activity. I know when Sam has had sugar during the day immediately she arrives home and guess a wakeful night is ahead. Honey is a valuable alternative. You will find which particular foods your young person thrives on, which 'quirks' of eating are actually beneficial and which substances to avoid. Don't forget to feed yourself as well as possible for your own well-being!

1. Brewster, D. P. *You Can Breastfeed Your Baby Even in Special Situations,* Rodale Press, Emmaus, Pennsylvania. 1979 pp 125 – 244.

2. Ibid, pp 338 – 353.

The young visually handicapped child

# 12

# The Young Visually-Handicapped Child

LYNDSEY:

Vision is our most important sense. Seventy per cent of the stimulus to a baby's development comes from sight, and vision in the immediate post-natal period modifies brain development. Normally a baby learns to do things by observing others and then imitating. Vision is the biggest reason for movement; a baby rolls over and crawls in order to reach the toy he can see.

Vision is rich in information, it is continuous and provides a more complete stimulus than any other sense. It backs up the input from the other senses and provides a meaning to the world.

The child with a visual handicap, whatever the degree or reason, has problems; often visual impairment is accompanied by other handicaps. Vision is so important in the early years that without it developmental delay is inevitable. Why bother to hold up a heavy head when one does not receive the reward of seeing more for doing so? How to learn to speak if one cannot watch Mummy talking? Indeed, sight is a means of communication with others. It is harder to bond with a visually-handicapped baby because much of the early 'reward' system may be missing; a baby rewards Mum with a smile and eye contact that melts her heart and Mum smiles and gazes lovingly back into baby's eyes. The bonding process without vision does not happen so easily, and needs to be worked at. Lots of physical contact; cuddling, soothing, singing and crooning and careful handling will probably be needed. A baby sling may be helpful, so that the baby can be safe and close but so that Mum can have arms free. The immediate response that a mother receives from her child will not be so easily achieved and it is easy to feel that the rapport is missing. It is hard to bear but try not to be too despondent; try to maximise every little nuance from your child and keep working at it. It will come eventually, however badly handicapped the child, as you both become more tuned-in to each other.

It is much more difficult for the world to make sense and be an inviting and stimulating place for a child with little or no vision; often it is strange and frightening. Lots of reassurance, physical contact and guidance are needed to ensure that the child feels safe, happy and able to learn to participate.

This said, it is equally important that the visually-handicapped child is able to explore and learn by mistakes, just as a non-handicapped child is. It is very easy for parents to over-protect because of the handicap – if at all possible let a few tumbles and bangs occur, for these mean that the child is moving, experimenting and learning. Much of this movement will be done in a fairly controlled setting, with someone watching or helping or arranging a clear pathway or certain obstacles. If your child manages to move about on his own, it is a good idea to train yourself to say 'stop' when a danger is reached, rather than 'no', as 'stop' does not have the negative or 'naughty' connotation.

However little movement your child is capable of, it is important to try to encourage a feeling of physical freedom. Gross movement by the child may be impossible, but parents can teach the child not to be afraid of it by gradually introducing it into play. Some rough and tumble play each day, perhaps with Dad when he comes home from work, can gradually be built up until the child feels safe and confident enough to be thrown up into the air or to fall and be caught. With our own multiply-handicapped little boy we have found that rolling off the sofa has encouraged him to be more mobile generally. We placed cushions on the floor and at first helped him to roll off. He now does this step with little intervention from us; sometimes he bumps a bit too hard or gets stuck, but he finds it really exhilarating.

Many other ideas on movement will come from professionals involved with your child. A peripatetic teacher of the visually-impaired, a community paediatric physiotherapist or a Portage worker may be working with your child regularly. However, there are lots of activities to stimulate any residual vision or to compensate for the lack of vision that can be carried out quite simply and enjoyably at home. They just take time and patience.

In the following list I have tried to include a wide variety of ideas. Some, at least, should be useful for any child, whatever the degree of visual handicap and additional problems. I have set out the ideas under the headings of the five senses, but obviously many of the activities involve several, if not all, of the senses.

Don't feel guilty if it is difficult to get around to doing much in this line; even little will help and we all feel we could do much more with our children than we do. Remember that children need some time on their own too, times in which a child learns to play by himself and develop any inner resources he has. Try to make sure he will not be bored, but give him time to himself sometimes, and other periods of organised play.

Try not to make these organised activities too much of a chore, either for you or the child; learning through fun is better for both of you. Try to include other children too. Dig out the Christmas box, collect everybody else's junk and experiment. A house festooned with Christmas decorations in the middle of June may look odd to the neighbours but it's fairyland for children.

Have fun!

## VISION

The following ideas are designed to stimulate any scrap of vision that may be present. I have found that the best results are achieved by placing objects very close to my little boy's face, but you will need to experiment with this. Do be careful if the light source is very strong not to shine it directly into the child's eyes. The effect of many of these objects is enhanced by working in the dark (we shut ourselves in the cupboard under the stairs!) or by shining an anglepoise lamp or similar lamp directly onto the object. Try to keep other stimuli such as noise to an absolute minimum so that it is easier to assess whether or not the child's response is related to seeing.

*Objects with their own light source.* Pen light torch (with a very narrow beam); large torch consisting of white light, orange or red light and flashing light; toy torches with a variety of different-coloured plastic covers; candles and matches; sparklers, (the last three are not recommended for use in the cupboard under the stairs!): luminous self-adhesive stars that glow in the dark (my little boy has them on the wall right by his bed so that (I think) he can see them when in bed).[1]

*Shiny objects.* Note that different objects are appropriate to different age groups. Kitchen foil; shiny gift wrap; coloured cellophane; survival blanket (if you wrap the child in it don't let him get too warm); laser-cut discs (from gift shops); mirrors; mirror with bell attached for pet birds; foil trays for cooking; Christmas decorations of all sorts (but beware of sharp edges and fire-retardant finishes); party hats and blowers with shiny trims; shiny toy windmills on a stick; toy balls made of a translucent plastic containing glittery bits; jewellery; marbles; glass objects; cutlery; kitchen utensils; saucepans; metal bells; silver, brass or copper ornaments; water and coloured liquids in glass or plastic bottles (food colouring or fluorescent paint from model shops); crystals (from gift shops); glitter.

Hang objects on a frame or in the window or doorway, or light objects from the lampshade suspended on a wire coathanger.

*Objects giving contrast/pattern.* Contrast can be the most important aspect of vision, more meaningful than colour or light. A person or an object can often be seen more clearly against the light so that they are in relief. Positioning oneself between the child and the window, for instance when feeding, may be effective.

Keep rooms light: throw away the net curtains!

Black patterns on white, or vice versa, and small, regular, repeating patterns may be seen more clearly than colours and random patterning, for example on fabric, wallpaper and gift wrap.

A board covered in matt black fabric with bright objects such as a shiny spoon and a yellow plastic cup attached to it using Velcro spots. Held or propped up in front of the child this contrast can help the child to find the objects.

## HEARING

This will probably be the most important sense for many visually-handicapped children. Sound will be used to locate objects, people and places (a blind adult can tell the comparative size and shape of a room by the quality of sound in the room). Objects that make a noise, either by themselves or when handled by the child, will be very important. There are obviously lots of toys that will come into this category, but everyday objects, both in and outside the home, will probably be very instructive and enjoyable to your child. Wooden spoons on tin lids, the ticking of a watch, door bells, telephones (so many different sounds these days!), the key in the lock when Daddy comes home, the bath water running, the clink of milk bottles, the factory siren... all these noises, if explained, will give pleasure to your child and help him to place things and times of the day.

Above all, the human voice takes on even more importance when vision is lacking. It is very important to talk to any child, but it is vital to talk to a child without sight. Always warn your child when you are about to handle him, tell him what you are about to do and then describe the garment about to be put on, talk about his body as you touch it, discuss the food about to be eaten, "label" objects and people and places, talk to him as you work, tell him what his baby brother is doing and how bright the sunshine is. All of this is much easier if you are naturally a talkative person (our household is so verbose that it is hard to get a word in edgeways!) but try to make it a habit and pretty soon you will be receiving odd looks as you describe what you are doing in the supermarket when your child is not even present! In the midst of this torrent of words do remember to leave gaps in which your child can answer and wait long enough for a response, as this may take some time if thought processes are slow. Ask questions, too, so that a response is required and the words may then become a conversation rather than a monologue. My own little boy has no speech but now always answers questions in a meaningful way.

The speech of, or noises made by, other children and babies is important too, and also the speech or sounds made by the handicapped child himself; a tape recording of the child or of other children is very effective.

The rhythms of singing, rhymes and story reading or telling can be very soothing. Songs and rhymes also aid hand games and movement and make physiotherapy more fun.

Wind chimes.

Musical boxes, toy musical instruments, variety of rattles.

Saucepans and kitchen utensils.

Cutlery.

Foil dishes, especially when suspended from a frame with string make a very satisfying sound when hit with a wooden spoon.

Cake and biscuit tins.

Packets of crisps.

Bells: all shapes and sizes and tones, including ornamental brass ones; tiny ones from pet shops attached to ribbon and put around the child's wrists and ankles to encourage movement; stitched onto clothing or an apron; bells inside soft toy cubes; doorbells; shop door bells; church bells etc.

Music: live and recorded. Try to vary the styles and volume.

Musical instruments: mouth organ; gazoo; tambourine; drum; maraccas; castanets; hand bells; triangle.

Telephones.

Motors: hoover; washing machine; electric drill; central heating; lawn mower; etc.

Fire engines; police cars; trains; cars; reversing bleepers on lorries and buses; the dustbin lorry; factory sirens; etc.

Water: running taps; splashing; washing-up; boiling liquids; fizzy drinks; blowing bubbles through a straw or with squeezy containers.

Food cooking, especially frying. My little boy loves the sound of sausages sizzling in the pan (seems to work up an appetite too!).

Natural sounds: birds singing; trees in the wind; dead leaves; the sea; running water; hail; etc.

In the midst of this cacophony of sound don't forget the value of silence and the need for quiet times, especially before bed time. Be sparing in the use of radio and television: they are fine at certain times but as continual background will merely confuse and mask other sounds.

## TOUCH

This will be very important to a visually-handicapped child. The following ideas are useful, but don't forget that the most important form of touching for a developing child is that of physical contact with other people's bodies and with his own body. We all need to be touched, frequently and consistently, in a loving and respectful manner. The visually-handicapped child will need this even more. He will need the reassurance of familiar bodies to give him a feeling of safety, he will need through touch the sense of being loved or praised that he will not pick up from a tender glance or a beaming smile and he will need help to feel his own body in order to build up his own body image. If you cannot see your feet and hands or your face in the mirror it needs effort to know where 'me' begins and ends and what 'me' is like. Lots of 'naming' and touching the parts of the body can be done to rhymes and songs, and washing and dressing are particularly important times for this. It is a good idea to touch the part of the body about to be washed or clothed before doing so, e.g. touch one foot and say "now we'll put on your sock" and then put on the sock.

Tickling, kissing, licking and blowing on various parts of the body are great fun for all concerned, as well as being instructive. A paintbrush or pastry brush gives a pleasant sensation. Mouths are particularly sensitive. A visually-handicapped child may use his mouth to explore objects long after the time when a normal child would do this.

Rougher physical play can be encouraged too, but needs to be eased into – to be thrown up into the air could be terrifying for a child with no sight. However, it's important to encourage gross movement and not to 'cotton wool' your child too much.

Here are some ideas for 'feeling':

*Textures*. Fabrics: silk, knobbly tweeds; raised patterns; knitting; fur (many visually-handicapped children are uneasy about this); shiny fabrics; sacking; suede; felt; etc. Papers – sandpaper; foils; coarse sugar paper; cellophane; tissue paper; loo paper; corrugated cardboard; bubble plastic.

*Toys*. Playmats; Lego and Duplo; Sticklebricks; 'Playskool' padded textured toys (monkey, ball etc.); 'Feely' books and 'Scratch 'n' Sniff' books (a story that has objects to feel, or to smell, within each illustration). Home made feely books are fun – perhaps Granny or a friend would make one. Make a cloth book out of different types of fabric and incorporate shells, feathers, brooches, milk bottle tops, pockets, press studs, strings and ribbons, small fabric animals, squeakers, (from haberdashers or sewing shops) etc. Feely boards – different papers and textures stuck onto a board that can be propped in front of the child or attached to his chair or tray. Egg boxes; polystyrene; empty cartons; tin full of cleaned milk bottle tops, especially if you can get different coloured tops. This makes a nice noise when shaken but is lovely to run the fingers through and finally tip out all over the child (yes, Mum gets to pick them all back up again!)

Floor coverings: carpets; mats; vinyl; cork; rush matting; door mats; dhurries; floorboards etc. These all make different noises too.

Bowls of pulses, rice, pasta, flour, sand, fruit, table-tennis balls, marbles.

Sandpit.

Water: often a wonderfully liberating medium, even for the child who hates to be washed. Bath time, with lots of warm relaxing water, bubbles, toys, straws and empty squeezy bottles with which to blow bubbles, can be explorative whilst being great fun.

Bowls of water, both inside and in the garden, provide lots of opportunity for learning and pleasure.

The swimming pool is enjoyed by almost all children, however badly handicapped, eventually. (My little boy took months and months of gentle persuasion to tolerate the pool, but now adores it.)

Massage can be very rewarding and enjoyable for both people concerned. If the child tolerates being touched he will probably learn to enjoy a session of massage and end up relaxed and soothed. It is also very soothing for the "masseur" or "masseuse" and is a lovely intimate time that can bring you and the child closer together. Remember to have warm hands and a warm room, choose a peaceful time of the day and remove as much of the child's clothing as is practical or will be tolerated. Experiment with different media to facilitate light massaging movements and to provide pleasant or stimulating smells, such as scented oils, talcum powder, creams and lotions, Body Shop preparations (Raspberry Ripple massage cream and Peppermint foot lotion).

Animals: pets or visits to zoos and farms can provide lots of fun and education too (not only to touch the animals but to hear them and smell them too).

## SMELL

Many of these ideas merge the sense of smell with that of taste. Be careful with very strong-smelling substances so as not to "jolt" the child too much.

Foodstuffs: obviously there are hundreds of possibilities here, but some of the more obvious are herbs and spices, coffee, pickles, fruit, onions, wine, fresh baking, yeast etc.

Perfumes: soaps; toothpaste; shaving cream; pot pourri; disinfectant; kitchen and bathroom cleansers; etc.

Outside: flowers; wet soil; newly mown grass; the dustbin; the compost heap; the car; the petrol station; the bakery; the cowshed; etc. Some parks such as the one in the middle of Winchester, have scented gardens specially laid out for the blind and in raised beds for easy access by wheelchair.

Toys: the Early Learning Centre make soft, squeaky, vinyl toys that are scented with vanilla.

Aroma disc: this is a small box into which can be inserted a selection of discs providing different smells (such as lavender, Christmas, woodland, etc.). The box then wafts the aroma around the room.

You may like to make some little fabric sachets and fill them with such things as lavender, cloves, nutmeg, ginger, vanilla pods or the little wooden balls used to scent drawers. These can then be used as they are under the child's nose or tucked into pockets or sewn onto an apron. (An apron can also be used with other objects attached: bells; squeakers (from sewing shops); piece of chain; velvet ribbon; scraps of cloth; a small spoon; a piece of sponge; a key ring; etc. so that the child can find them.)

*TASTE*

Many of the ideas under smell will also feature here. Try to make food varied
and interesting in taste, texture and smell because much of the pleasure of eating
lies in the sight of it. Do try your child occasionally with some 'naughty' things
such as fizzy drinks, sherbet and ice-cream. We have found that we need to warn
our little boy if the food is going to be very cold or if it will bubble up in his
mouth and once warned he really enjoys the novel experience.

I hope that this list is not too daunting but will furnish some ideas to get you
going. I am sure that you will have lots of ideas of your own as you start to work
with your child in this way, and that you will also pick up ideas from other
parents. Try to explore lots of avenues to compensate for the lack of sight but
not to give up on any residual vision. Most of these activities will just seem like
play and fun to your child but will be helping him a great deal.

Jim, Lyndsey, Jesse and Laurie

Laurie

Deafness in childhood

# 13

## Deafness in Childhood

The following is a resumé of two conversations with Susanna Burnett, and her grown daughter, Catherine, who was born with deafness due to the rubella suffered by her mother during pregnancy.

SUSANNA:

I first noticed my daughter's hearing loss in early infancy. Our family doctor referred us to a hospital hearing clinic. The tests included using crinkly paper, rattles or other noise-producing toys, to see if the baby would respond. Because Catherine still had some residual hearing, and was an intelligent baby able to react to any visual clues, the tests only demonstrated that she had some hearing, but not the degree of her hearing loss. The hospital staff told me I was "making a fuss," and sent us away. As Catherine developed from a baby into a toddler, I noticed that she wasn't babbling; then she did not begin to say words at the right time. When she was rising three, I took matters into my own hands again, and took Catherine to the Great Ormond Street Children's Hospital for further testing. The professionals there, who have a lot of experience with children of different degrees of deafness, could see immediately that she was deaf. There Catherine was finally fitted with hearing aids, and together we went to the Nuffield Speech and Hearing Centre in London for a week's intensive training in how to cope with the hearing aid, and to reorganise ourselves to make the best use of her residual hearing.

When she reached school age, I took the step of putting her into a normal school, in conjunction with regular therapy on the side. For her it was the best choice, as she has formed strong friendships with her classmates, and has enjoyed a normal life, despite her handicap. It was a gamble at the time, but it has been well worth it. Catherine is now attending college, studying graphic design.

My advice to other parents in similar situations is: follow your own intuition and have your baby's hearing tested *as early as possible* if you suspect a hearing loss. If there is any question of deafness, the 8–9th month is extremely important. It is then that a child will react most spontaneously to sounds, and does not yet have the toddler's wariness of strangers or new situations which might confuse test results at a later age. Don't accept a "wait and see" attitude from doctors or other professionals. Babies are now being fitted with hearing aids very early, and this can help a child tremendously to keep up with normal stages of speech development. Almost all children suffering from deafness can benefit from hearing aids, for it can help them to make maximum use of whatever residual hearing they've got. If your baby also suffers from other problems, and does not seem to respond normally to your voice, even though he seems to be startled at loud noises, then a hearing test might help to sort out why the baby is not responding. Children who are deaf often are labelled as stupid or even mentally retarded, because they may remain "in their own world" unless helped to communicate. They may also go in for a lot of temper tantrums out of sheer frustration. I found it helped Catherine a lot when she was a child, if I could actually show her and let her touch things when I was trying to explain something to her. I remember once she threw a tantrum because she wanted to wear her dressing gown. I tried to explain to her that I had washed it and that she couldn't wear it that evening because it was drying on the line. She only understood when I actually took her outside and let her feel the water dripping off it.

Once a child has been fitted with hearing aids, it is essential that he wear them *all* the time. It will be of no use at all in the drawer! It can be extremely hard to make a rebellious toddler wear a hearing aid; but it is very important to insist it be worn, from the very first day. A child with deafness can feel very isolated and cut off from what is happening. As parents we can help by talking to our child about everything that is going on – telling the child about what people are saying, describing what the child sees so he can learn the words for everyday objects, reading to the child. Even though he may not be able to hear, it will help him learn to read your lips. Lip-reading, along with other forms of communication, will be the key for him to learn to communicate with others. Remember also that you cannot warn your child of danger by calling to him! This is especially important in early childhood when the child is learning about his environment. You will need to keep close by your child, especially in dangerous situations, like when crossing the road, or in the kitchen or by the fire.

It helps to know that even very modern hearing aids are only crude substitutes for natural hearing. Unlike glasses, which can be tailored to meet a wide variety of visual defects, hearing aids can only amplify sound. It would be like giving magnifying glasses to everyone with a sight problem, regardless of whether they are nearsighted or farsighted. Often a child can hear some sounds quite well, but others not at all. Some of the newest hearing aids are beginning to be able to differentiate high sounds and low sounds, but the technology is still very awkward, compared with glasses. And unfortunately there is still a stigma attached to wearing a hearing aid. This is a pity, since people have long since become accustomed to seeing children wearing glasses. As parents we need to have an optimistic, matter-of-fact attitude towards the hearing aid; this will help our child to accept it as a fact of everyday life.

## CATHERINE:

One of my earliest memories after I had my first hearing aids, is of a nosy lady who asked me if I was listening to music on my little radio. "No," I said, "it's my hearing aid". Was she ever embarrassed! When we went on holiday at the seaside, and now when I go swimming in a pool, I have to take out my hearing aids. As a child, this meant my mother had to come into the water after me, because I couldn't hear her calling me to come out. Now, even though I enjoy the feel of the water, I can sometimes feel very cut off from what's around me.

On the whole, I have enjoyed going to school with hearing classmates. However, in my last few years of secondary school, especially as I began preparing for exams, it became more and more difficult. Since I had to watch the teacher's face all the time in order to lip-read, I found it impossible to take notes at the same time. I had to do a lot of extra reading to make up for what I couldn't jot down during class, as well as often having to ask my classmates if I could borrow their notes.

It helps me to lip-read if the person who is speaking goes slowly, speaks clearly, and uses simple phrases. Since it's so important for me to be able to see their face, it helps me if the speaker faces towards the light, and doesn't talk while eating or smoking. Conversations between several people are difficult for me to follow, because I don't always know who will speak next, and I can't always see everyone's face. If a friend clues me in when the conversation changes subject, this helps me to pick up the thread again. Contrary to popular opinion, it is absolutely no help at all when someone shouts; it only makes matters worse.

It's great to be at college now, though I am meeting a completely new situation. Many people I meet for the first time don't know about my deafness. Sometimes I need to tell them so they won't misinterpret my reactions, for instance, if I don't greet them, when I haven't heard them say hello to me. Despite many difficulties, I am optimistic for the future.

Sleep

# 14

## *Sleep*

JENNI:

Sleep is one of the most frequently expressed stress areas for families whose children have handicaps. It's as if the process of falling asleep and waking up were fundamentally bound up with the state of handicap itself. A child cannot wake up in the morning, or has kept weary parents up most of the night, or sleeps fitfully, never really relaxing into restorative deep sleep. During the day, even after a wakeful night, one child may be full of energy, though the parents can barely cope, they're so exhausted. Another child may indeed manage to sleep well and deeply at night, but remain half asleep and lethargic during the day. Then a child who has experienced epileptic fits may also be on anticonvulsant medicines which help keep the fits under control, but also keep the child in a slightly sedated state all the time.

The variations of sleep problems are as numerous as children themselves. However, through listening to the experience of a great many parents, and reflecting on our own experiences I think that sleep problems generally seem to fall into two categories, and might be characterized by two sorts of pictures. The first is of a child who when awake is lethargic and never seems really to "wake up" completely. Though he or she might be afflicted by many different sorts of handicaps, the child would probably be very slow in motor milestones and not have attained much independence in movement or activities during the day. (This might be a child with hydrocephalus, or athetoid cerebral palsy, or some forms of brain damage and resulting severe mental delay caused by birth injury, but where there is muscle laxness rather than spasticity.) During the day, unless given constant stimulation and physical contact and movement the child tends to sit or lie where he is put and not do anything. When bedtime comes and the child is put to bed, he naturally has a hard time falling asleep because lying in bed seems (or so I imagine) like a continuation of the daytime experience of doing nothing. Perhaps the child cries, either during the day, from boredom, or during the night, from sleeplessness. The child's crying may make the situation tense emotionally for the parents, because they know and can feel their child's frustration and boredom during the day, will have tried to entertain as much as possible, yet will also have had all the other tasks of daily life to cope with at the same time during the day. Meanwhile, it's now late at night, the child cannot fall asleep and the parents themselves are tired. Through one means or another the little one finally does fall into deep sleep, perhaps even sleeping quite late in the morning, or as late as it is allowed.

The parents may be tempted just to let the child sleep as long as possible. Then the evening comes round again and the whole cycle plays itself through again. If the situation becomes extreme the child may hardly be awake at all in the day, may be driving parents crazy with sleeplessness at night, and no one is coping very well with other tasks in life.

The other extreme is the child who is "too awake" all of the time, though this awakeness might not necessarily be in a useful way. This sort of child might be suffering from severe spastic cerebral palsy, and have most of his muscles tensed up during the day; or the child might have autism or some other personality disorder, and be haunted with repetitive movements or questions or thought sequences when awake; or the child might be suffering from eczema or severe allergies which it experiences as painful itching or as a kind of exaggerated sense awareness, to the point of an all-over experience of physical or sensorial pain; or the child might be particularly excitable, vulnerable to loud noises and bright lights, frightened to the point of screaming by new situations, people, places. Such children may also have great difficulty in falling asleep, or even in staying in their bed. They may cry a great deal, both in the evenings while trying to fall asleep, and during the night, between periods of sleep. Naturally the tensions rise very quickly, as the child gets more and more distressed, both from tiredness and from sensory overload, and the parents get more and more upset with the noise, the incessant demands upon them and their own fatigue.

In both sorts of sleep problems it may be that some solutions can be found not only in the actual bedtime ritual but also in the way the child's day experiences are planned for. It has become common knowledge today that a person's experiences during the day have a significant effect upon the quality of their sleep, and this is even more evident with children with handicaps. Frequently parents reach a kind of numbed state of resignation about their child's sleep disturbances because they have not been helped to differentiate between what may be inherent in their child's condition, and what they can change in their home routines and environment to help their child sleep *despite* the handicapping condition.

Looking again at the first picture, the sort of child who has difficulty ever really "waking up", it may be very helpful for the parents to sit down and actually plan a daily timetable – perhaps with the help of a professional person who has frequent contact with the child – where they plan for structured, meaningful activity for the child and who will carry out the activity, and how it will fit into the timetable of the rest of the family. Given that there may be the needs of brothers and sisters to consider, plus pressures of work and the many necessary household chores, this may be an area where you'll find it useful to turn to different secondary sources of help. If your toddler would benefit from fresh air every day, there must be someone in the community who would take her for a walk regularly if you cannot. (See "How to Get Help".) Try to plan definite play, story, or music times.

If you are satisfied that the child has a healthy daily routine, you may also wish to seek the advice of someone – perhaps a professional (health visitor, G.P., child psychologist), family friend or relative with lots of parenting experience, to help sort out which part of the child's sleep problem seems to be *part of* the handicap and which is a question of "bedtime parenting skills" – skills which can be learned and improved upon. Sometimes by looking at ways of managing the child's sleep routine, parents can incorporate new approaches which – though they wouldn't do away with the problems inherent in the child's handicap – may well bring the situation generally more under control so that though the handicap remains, the sleeping pattern gradually becomes bearable.

Bedtime routine might include a story, some cuddling, some singing (yes even if the parents feel they can't sing, a real live human voice singing, even off key, is very soothing and certainly shows the child that you care about him or her more than being put to bed with a machine playing fancy music). If the parents wish, a prayer could be said. In our home we have always sung to the children by candlelight, which seems to have a very quieting effect. I suggest that it may help a child not to watch television just before bed, nor listen to loud recorded music, as both of these are activities which would tend to wake them up rather than quieten them for sleep. Make the area around the child's bed as beautiful and calm as possible. Obviously tastes differ, but I would suggest that soft colours and pretty pictures to look at by the bed might help sleep, rather than loud posters of popular culture idols or potentially frightening images from space fantasy films or robotic toys or the like.

Keeping the noise down in the rest of the house just after bedtime could also help the child to fall asleep. This doesn't mean that all life must completely stop, but only that as adults we be a little sensitive about how much noise is reaching, and perhaps distracting, our child.

In the case of a child who is too "awake", though perhaps in not a normal way, not only the actual content of the day's experiences will have an effect upon sleep, but also *how* the day's activities are actually carried out. It may be helpful in such a case for the parents to look at *how much*, and *what kind* of stimulation the child is getting during the day. Parents of children with handicaps are often told to "stimulate" their child as a way of helping development. And whereas this may be useful advice in some ways, it needs to be done carefully, and is not a matter of merely subjecting the child indiscriminately to whatever stimulation is around, with no thought to its *quality*.

There are many different kinds of stimulation. First, there is the stimulation of all the senses – sight, sound, smell, touch, taste – there is also what could be called "emotional stimulation", and "atmosphere-stimulation". I believe that for all children, and most especially for children with handicaps who show signs of over-excitement or sensory overload, it is very important to give to the child the right quality of stimulation, while protecting her from "overload" or "loud" stimulation. There is an important distinction between what is *real* and what is *canned*. For example, for visual stimulation, taking a child out into nature – perhaps a garden in bloom – rather than watching telly. Or on a rainy day, to look at picture books or magazines, or do painting or colouring, or even, in a quiet moment – perhaps during naptime? – to open the window and draw the curtains so the wind can move the curtains and the sunlight can shine through the pretty pattern on the cloth. Does the child hear real and harmonious music, however simple? Is she exposed to pleasant smells – fresh flowers, pot pourri, bath salts or herbal drinks – which help counter-balance the smells of traffic or smoke? Are there some environments of glare, crush and noise that are best avoided?

The age-old remedy of a warm bath and a cup of warm milk just before bedtime also can sometimes help. Adding an infusion of lavender herb tea can bring a pleasant smell and have a calming effect. (Health food shops generally carry a wide selection of herb teas as well as books on herbal remedies.) If your child suffers from cold feet, then a warm foot bath just before bed and woolly socks on over his pyjamas might help falling asleep. For very young children, a real woollen fleece to lie on can be a great comfort.

Finally, no child – whether wakeful, sleepy, or "in–between" will sleep well at night if they are uncomfortable, in pain, or having difficulty breathing. The physiotherapist can help with positioning for a little one that is safe and relaxing. In our personal case, a cranial osteopath has been very helpful. Avoid all sedating medications except in the most extreme or dire situation. If a pattern of sleep is to be maintained on a rhythmical and reliable basis it must be established naturally.

HOLLY:

The time leading into sleep is one of the most important events in the child's day. It is a time of transition. The child can be helped to let go of all the day's experiences and to live for a moment with his own inner peace. It is a time for feeling the secure embrace of unconditional love from his parents and the angels above. In this way we can help create a sleep which is rejuvenating for the child, rather than troubled.

In our family we begin preparing for sleep after dinner. All of us join together to clear the table and to put the toys back into their homes. This putting away and making order of the day's work is an important outward image of the order we are trying to help our children achieve inwardly. Jeff and I do most of the putting away. Naomi puts away a few things, while Benjamin follows and takes them out again! However, with humour and with patience, we get the job done. Of course, there is sometimes a very special project, like a bakery we have created, with a table, cloths, pans, dishes, mud pies, grass tea and pretend money, which we will want to leave for the next day. Usually, however, it is much more fun to begin anew each morning.

After the children are helped into their night clothes, Mama, Papa, Naomi and Benjamin go into the bedroom, which has been prepared for the night with curtains drawn, lights out and a candle lit. The four of us, with Naomi's baby doll, Rachel, sit on the floor in a circle and listen to Papa or Mama play a gentle melody on the lyre. Sometimes Naomi or Benjamin also play a song on the lyre.

The song leads us to a short activity done purely for the joy of interacting together in play. We continue the activity in the form of a circle and keep it as uncomplicated and as peaceful as possible. We do the same activity every night for about six weeks, with minor changes to keep it living. Various activities have been creating a short puppet show, using the dolls and stuffed animals at hand. Or I might tell a story I have created especially for the children, using simple eurythmy[1] gestures which the children follow. One of the children's favourites is to play little finger games.

After our activity, Naomi tells Rachel about her day. This is a wonderful way to hear what stood out for Naomi and how it affected her. It also gives all of us an opportunity to remember together, to talk things over and to bring about a resolution to the day. Having the conversation directed to a doll helps to make it less personal. Rachel is a most loving, objective observer.

After remembering the day together, Jeff and I sing a lullaby to the children. Still in a circle, we put our hands together and say a prayer for Benjamin. We then say a prayer for Naomi, who joins us as best she can. The children are helped into their beds, kisses and hugs are given, and the candle is blown out.

### Benjamin's Prayer[2]
(Prayer for quite small children spoken by a grown–up.)

May light stream into you, that can take hold of you.
I follow its rays with the warmth of my love.
I think with my thinking's best thoughts of joy
On the stirrings of your heart.
Thoughts to strengthen you,
Thoughts to cleanse you.
I want to gather my thoughts of joy
Before the steps of your life,
That they bind themselves to your will for life,
So that it finds itself with strength
In all the world,
Ever more,
Through itself.

*Naomi's Prayer*[2]
(Prayer for little children who themselves already pray.)

From my head to my feet
I'm the image of God
From my heart to my hand
I feel his breath.
When I speak with my mouth
I shall follow God's will
When I see and know God
In my Mama and Papa
In all loving people
In birds, beasts, plants and stones
No fear shall I feel
Only love can surround me
For all that is around me.

1. Eurythmy is a form of movement and expressive dance.

2. From *Prayers for Mothers and Children,* by Rudolf Steiner.

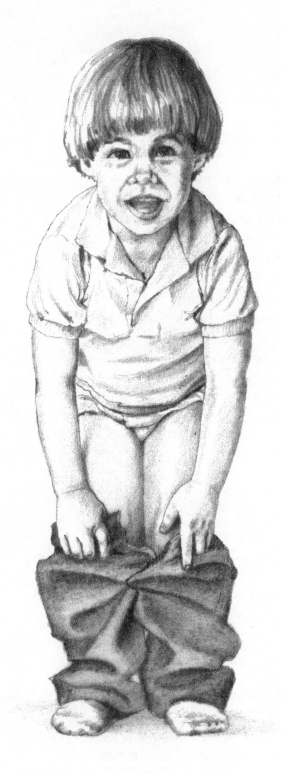

Clothing

# 15

## *Clothing*

JENNI:

The thoughtful dressing of a child with a handicap can help to minimize the *impression* of disability presented to other people, thus helping the child and ourselves to feel more confident and self-assured. Keeping high standards means doing our best to see that clothes are mended, clean and suitable. It does not mean we need spend a lot of money on new clothes or have a cupboard overflowing with the latest fashions. It is more a question of choosing styles which look pleasing on the child. Many of us go to jumble sales or receive clothes from friends' children. Wearing second hand clothing need not be a bad thing – it is all a question of choosing the articles which look good and passing along the others. If we are able to afford new clothes for our child, that is nice. But expensive clothes do not guarantee good style – that remains a question of choosing wisely to enhance the child's looks, and not necessarily dressing him in the trendy clothes which fill some shops.

It can help the child's personality to shine through if we are careful not to overwhelm with clothing with large printed slogans on the front or cartoon figures of questionable taste which risk mocking the child's unattractive features – drooling, droopy eye-lids, irregular features, etc. – through the cartoonist's caricature of the human face. It may be most flattering to an introverted child to wear softer colours with smaller patterns, whereas a more extroverted child might look very good in very bright colours and bold patterns. It is really a question of gaining a sense, through observation, of what becomes the child most, in terms of both colour, pattern and style, and try to make the best use of what is most attractive.

All children get dirty during the normal course of the day, and with a "normal" child it doesn't matter so much because the dirt is an expression of the child's experiencing life to the full and his personality shines through the "grit and grime". A child with a handicap tends to get dirty in a different way – often because of lack of control of body functions – and his personality may have a hard job to shine through the dirt. A child with handicap may tend to sink into grubbiness until it begins to define him, rather than the reverse. Keeping the child clean means not only regular baths and shampoos, it also means keeping shoes shined, glasses wiped, hair combed, wheelchairs or pushchairs scrubbed and noses wiped. If drooling is a problem then bibs need to be changed frequently so they don't begin to smell; the same goes for nappies. It may help to use an extra bit of perfume or body-care products – not to replace washing, of course, but to freshen up the child in between washes (scented wipes are good for faces, a bit of cologne on the brush freshens the hair, some talcum powder keeps the body dry and comfortable). Teeth may need extra attention, even brushing after each meal, both to prevent decay (dental work may mean a general anaesthetic), and to keep the mouth fresh. Hair styled neatly, and attractively is a lovely "boost" to appearance.

It is a good idea to adopt clothing which suits the child's real age group, rather than his developmental age group: Though a child with profound retardation may stay at the early infant developmental level for a long time, it can help us and others who meet the child (and of course the child himself!) to be conscious of his real age, enhancing a sense of maturing personality, if we dress him at his real age level. This means both evolving towards new styles (that is clothing shapes) and different patterns of decoration. Prints of nursery animals give way to more sophisticated patterns, little-girl smocked dresses become skirts and blouses or adult-style dresses, boys' trousers no longer have elasticated waists but zippers and waistbands, etc. To a certain extent these changes will occur naturally as the child's size grows and fashions evolve from one age group to another. But often parents are called upon to choose between different options, and keeping in mind the child's real age can help. This may mean also avoiding dressing our teenaged daughter in outdated hand-me-downs – even if they are still in excellent repair – because these may be too *old* for the adolescent's real age.

If a wheelchair or other appliance is used, it can be kept clean and even decorated with attractive, coloured cushions, pleasant decals or other personal touches. This can add another touch of dignity to help the child live up to his or her full potential.

By doing our utmost as parents to dress our children attractively, maintaining high standards of cleanliness (and repair), fashion and appropriateness (to age and personality) we are making a strong statement to the world about our convictions: the importance of human dignity, the value of our child's life and the place he or she has in society. Keeping up our child's standards of appearance also tells the world clearly how much we are proud of our childs' achievements, (however small they may seem to us sometimes), and how we value human *qualities* above physical or mental "perfection."

*Dress your child up towards what you would like him to achieve,* rather than down towards what his condition seems to dictate.

Play

# 16

# *Play*

HOLLY:

Naomi has a very difficult time playing on her own. At home, she invariably wants to do what I, or the adult nearby, is doing, and tends always to be on top of that person. As much as possible, I try to include her in my daily activities. When I prepare breakfast, Naomi's task might be to butter the toast. When I dust, Naomi also dusts. Even when we go to the grocery store, Naomi and I prepare our grocery lists together. Naomi's list includes four or five items which she is in charge of getting. This helps keep Naomi occupied, as well as focused, while we shop.

Naomi cannot hold her interest long enough to listen to any of the stories in her story books. We have found that very short made-up stories are the only stories in which Naomi will become involved. Naomi's favourites are the stories about a little girl – just like Naomi! If we make up stories using Naomi's dolls and puppets – all the better! In this way Naomi, too, can become involved as she takes on the role of one of the characters. We can become very elaborate and create a whole scene, using coloured cloths, stones, sea shells and bark. We even add musical accompaniment. Often Naomi wants to repeat the same puppet show again and again. If I leave out a part, she is the first to remember.

One activity Naomi, Benjamin and I thoroughly enjoy is cooking. Even when Benjamin, at eighteen months old, did nothing but sit like a Buddha all day, staring at his hands and the people around him, I would bring my dinner preparations down on the floor to his level and begin to chop, mix and pour. At first Benjamin was mildly interested in all this activity. Gradually, he began reaching out to touch things, and now he is so totally involved that he will sit in the mixing bowl if I am not careful!

We know that children learn through play, and we want our children to learn.

However, toys and activities that are for three to five-year-olds are often way beyond my five-year-old's ability. I am therefore, given the opportunity really to observe my child. What does she enjoy doing? Where? How? When? Play gives me the opportunity to meet her where she is. I can enter her world.

During Benjamin's Buddha stage (until age two), he would sit on the floor and rock for hours at a time. Sometimes I would sit beside him and rock, too. He would laugh and wiggle his fingers and toes in sheer delight. I was acknowledging and sharing in his play. Gradually, we added singing (I would sing; Benjamin sort of squealed) to the rocking, and then came clapping. Together we created our own game, initiated completely by Benjamin. We laughed and laughed over our game.

This brings up another essential characteristic of play. When I am playing with Benjamin or Naomi, and it is not joyful, I stop. Play should be fun! It can sometimes be frustrating when the children cannot or will not do what I have taken such trouble to plan. When this happens, I try to take a break from the activity and think over what went wrong. Oftentimes my expectations were too high. Other times my child was hungry or tired and didn't have the words or gestures to tell me. By thinking it through, I begin to learn more about my child. Through play I am able to gain more insight into my child's experience of the world so that I can help him unfold all that is in him.

## PADDY:

Play is so much a part of learning that when I saw over many months that my child couldn't and didn't play, I was very troubled. This was exacerbated by outsiders' comments and 'experts' who said you must teach her to play! I spent hundreds of hours with her introducing stimulations of all sorts and spent hundreds of pounds on toys of every conceivable type. But she did not ever 'play' in the accepted sense. I worried, fussed and sought advice and gradually ways to help her emerged. I pass them on keenly – knowing how valuable this knowledge was to me – and how hard it was to glean. Because each child is so different, self-help is really the only way to tackle this subject.

Sam was without interest in things happening around her or in the soft toys offered. She was content to sit. She reacted neither to sights nor sounds. I started to research and came up with:

A. Not all non-handicapped play by any means, and how and when they play is an individual matter. They often prefer to make up games and fashion toys from their own imagination, even from the earliest months.

B. Much (indeed all) of the 'play' suggested for babies/children is too complicated. Many experts simply don't realise how simple it has to be.

So this is how I started:

Whenever possible I held Sam in my arms as I went about the house, shopping, etc. and talked about what ever was around. I showed her movement (pushing the plates across the table, the cheese across the counter), and noise (a spoon in a glass) I ran and jumped and hopped holding her and she jigged up and down. Much of the time she didn't respond but it seemed instinctively right.

We stroked, tickled, kissed her soft toys and then we did the same to Sam. The first time she ever reacted to a toy was at three and a half years when she looked straight at a rubber Mickey Mouse and picked it up and cuddled him. A great day! We've always had a Mickey of some sort around the house from that day – we owe him a lot.

A few minutes every hour was the time limit. Gradually it was increased, but illness, tiredness, or unease acted as a stop. Really Sam has never needed or responded to toys. She slowly disclosed the things that interested her, like sticks, spoon, 2 inch high tiny pencil tops. She always has a collection to hand, even today. One day, aged five, she spent three quarters of an hour putting logs in and out of the log basket.

From the earliest times singing and reciting nursery rhymes has been a favourite play activity. She knows them all by heart and listens intently – still.

She can't bear sad songs and cries when she hears them. Tinkling or sharp noises alarm her, as do chiming clocks, bead curtains, shells strung to catch the wind and some musical instruments. Play has always had to accommodate her fears.

Books were always important, the Ladybird publications the right size for her hand. Start by talking about the pictures, not worrying about concentration because turning over pages helps make books good companions. I discouraged tearing but battered appearance meant they were loved objects. Television has never been of interest because we don't see much either; occasionally sitting with Father watching cricket and clapping the catches is fun.

Music is a main interest now and has been from pre-school times. After ten years teaching she has learned to use her own tape recorder or record player, a great step forward when it happened. Many youngsters, especially the autistic, are instinctively frightened of mechanical things. But learning to play their own music or tapes offers independence. There are a great many tapes collected over years, some as presents, and she chooses to suit her mood; not 'pop' but differing kinds including some spoken things. School years ago made tapes of class singing (very treasured) and I make tapes of nursery rhymes and poetry.

Sam never played with bricks or toy cars, ignored her dolls' house, disliked dolls till she was ten and even now only certain dolls are acceptable. She is fascinated by catalogues and spends hours poring over them, loves to be read to, knowing each story intimately and repeatedly asking for favourites. She recognises misplaced words and will stop the session until correction occurs.

Of course, all this is a simplification of the entire subject. I learned not to compare her with any other children for she went at her own rate. She never played with other childen but loved to watch their games. Water, sand and later finger paints were introduced from three onwards (it is a waste of time if they are not yet ready to experiment) though she didn't relax with them for years and play was generally throwing, splashing, eating, pushing around but as long as something happened it didn't matter.

Of activity play only swimming was popular and that immensely so, though again we took it in slow stages. Water in pools can be frightening and we learned then about *Danger*. "Be careful" "take care" had to be part of play situations in swimming pools, on swings, walking in roads or in the country. Play thus becomes a way of learning life skills – protecting yourself from hazards, finding that washing yourself, showering, bathing is essential but fun and that choosing clothes each day, or putting on shoes is about decision making.

Some further points about play. Youngsters become very attached to certain items which offer comfort and though we may not recognize them as conventional 'toys' they are vital to the security of their owners. Sam takes a bag with a collection of things everywhere and if parted from them becomes distraught. She also relaxes by running gravel or sand through her fingers sitting for hours in her own little world and that's her play. Teachers like to part her from her bag and gravel activities and I appreciate why, but if the bag goes completely you lose her co-operation. If, however, she can see it on a table or knows it is in a cupboard and will be returned at school end then she is relaxed. I am very mindful of this when I teach pupils who cling to treasured objects. A lesson for *us* to learn is that play is not just a way to pass time or to keep the youngsters out of the way for a while: it is the way in which they learn about themselves and the ways of the world in which they live.

Behaviour

# 17

## *Behaviour*

PADDY:

It is quite natural for parents to find times when they feel the need for guidance on how they should handle their handicapped youngsters' behaviour and perhaps the most useful thing to suggest is a balance between loving care which does not tip over into indulgence (too often) whilst also offering a disciplined structure to life which all children (despite their denials) find comforting.

These youngsters are no naughtier than others. They range easily through being sad, happy, tired, irritable, selfish, irritating, mischievous and lovable – the list is endless. They enjoy disobedience for the reactions it provokes and equally a bit of praise does wonders for them. For many handicapped children, their behaviour, i.e. their reaction to circumstances, is their only way of relating and inter-acting with others. If speech is limited, vocabulary small, movement difficult, what you do, how you react, co-operate or not is important and more important is that this reaction is understood for what it is. What is often labelled 'bad', 'noisy' or 'disturbed' is actually someone making a statement or needing attention and it is cruel and unhelpful of adults to use these labels.

Some handicapped youngsters do have tantrums, they do rage, throw themselves on the floor, spit and scream, but they are communicating. The adult recipient should calmly assess the meaning of these actions. At its simplest level the tantruming child may not want to go shopping because it is raining and he doesn't like wearing a mac. More seriously he may be very frightened of traffic and the swish of wheels through puddles or he may be tired and sickening for some illness. Sadly, he doesn't have the speech to explain this and that in itself is a frightening situation. We who are not frustrated by our physical inadequacies preventing us 'doing' or 'saying' can only imagine the pain of not being able to express our needs, hopes, and fears and excitements.

This does not mean that the handicapped shouldn't have to conform. They must expect to fit in as far as possible with the family, to play their part in its easy day-to-day running. A regular time for bed, for bathtime, for meals, gives a structure to their lives allowing that occasional illness or special treats will disrupt it more than a little. We ask too much of the handicapped, indeed deny them much if we do not allow them some struggles, some irritation at having to be unselfish, to experience other people's rejection of their ill-manners when they are exhibited.

It helps to know that if a youngster becomes too distraught or difficult to handle there are ways to change the situation. Peace and quiet are essential, so take them away from all distractions into a warm softly lit place. A warm bath at any time of day just to relax (no washing!) can be calming and a quiet cuddle and whispered gentle song can too. When things are fraught I whisper and curiosity at what I may be offering wins through. Alternatively, when a tantrum is in full swing I curl up in a ball on the floor and that too tempts Sam to investigate for she loves to laugh and Mum always unwraps with a giggle. Laughter is so infectious at any time.

All youngsters can pick their time to 'play-up' and however handicapped are quick to realise how embarrassed parents or carers feel if it happens in a shop or on a visit. Learn not to feel embarrassed for this is between you and the child and outsiders doubtless have had their moments with youngsters also. Be firm and insist on good behaviour and be determined to win provided the child really is being irritating and is not frightened, tired, in pain etc., in which case there are other remedies.

From early days balance love and kindness with showing the youngster that unruly and noisy behaviour is unacceptable because it distracts and troubles others. It is nothing to do with the handicap, simply that we all have to avoid making things too uncomfortable for people we are with.

There are times when parents need advice about aspects of a child's behaviour. If you find a psychologist, teacher or another parent with appropriate experience ask questions and discuss things – it helps because it can be worryingly difficult to decide if you are handling things well. There may not be a 'right' answer but there could be less misery for you.

*Self-Mutilation.* Self-mutilation is a distressing thing to encounter and it can start when children are quite small. Some bite themselves, knock their heads or limbs for long periods, others scratch or pick at places on their body. Sam bites her arm, always in the same place so it is often sore and sometimes bleeds. It happens when she becomes tense or frightened (by sudden noise for example) or if she is thwarted or believes she is not being understood. Of course it hurts (the onlooker as well as herself) but why self-mutilation happens is apparently not really understood though theories are advanced. By chance Sam is minus her front teeth which limits the damage – others aren't so fortunate.

How to cope is difficult to decide. Perhaps because of her particular syndrome she doesn't feel too much pain at the time or the resulting soreness. Perhaps this applies to other children too. Naturally we try to stop it, but we aren't always there nor is this easy for it makes her even more angry. And though certain things trigger Sam other children will have different reasons – difficult to fathom. Saying "It's wrong" has no effect, all one can do is calmly suggest "It's silly" and make sure the wound is kept clean. Just to add to the problem Sam refuses ever to have sticking plaster or ointment on her body. It is wise to be particularly careful about hygiene at all times. Sometimes, I have found scratching is minimised by keeping the areas soft by using body lotion.

*Temper Tantrums.* Once described by a visitor as World War III breaking out, these are shattering for parents and onlookers because they can be violent and youngsters with mental handicaps can be surprisingly swift in reactions and strong. Tantrums can't be ignored. Experience suggests that once known, avoiding the causes of such outbursts might help, though this begs the question of self-control. We make great efforts to prevent confrontations for the sake of furniture, ornaments and in the belief that firm calmness and a low-key approach to this problem is wisest.

When tantrums happen in shops and public places (and they do) Sam is removed as quickly as possible – not easy, especially if one parent is alone and I have bruises to prove it! Long observation of temper tantrums persuades me they are often beyond the true control of the youngster for the fury overwhelms them. They must come to understand, though, that this is not a method of getting their own way. At the end of the episode a period of sitting quietly or going into another room helps to quieten the atmosphere. The important thing is to have a coping routine that remains the same but it would be wrong to pretend tantrums are easily dealt with. They seem to increase in frequency and vigour at puberty but ease off in mid-twenties.

*Obsessive Behaviour.* Obsessive behaviour can continue for minutes or go into hours and the same routine persist for months or years. It is exhausting for the companion to endure, though the youngster doesn't appear to find it tiring or boring – in fact quite the reverse.

Sometimes it cannot be stopped so must be accepted.

Other times it is a comfort to the youngster when they are unsure and will stop when the stress lifts.

Another form of activity e.g. singing, walking, bathing, new toys may draw attention from the obsession.

Sam's obsessive rocking was deeply upsetting to me. I tried all the above remedies and sought advice. I can't say I ever found a reliable way to stop it but learned not to let it distress me. If she knocked herself as she rocked her position was moved. Gradually as the years passed it almost vanished appearing now only when she is not feeling well, and she will stop when asked. Some years ago she started to use her bed as a trampoline instead of rocking but naturally this is not encouraged.

The experience of most people seems to be that the obsessive behaviour fades over the years, but it may well be a very long process and not always complete. Is the problem perhaps, that we believe the obsession more harmful than it really is? I wonder.

*Words we would rather they hadn't picked up.* "Why," runs a frequently heard query, "do our youngsters – with among other things so little speech and supposedly not quick to learn, manage to pick up words not acceptable in polite society and remember them. Particularly when they remember so little else?" It's one of life's little mysteries. Sam did not speak until eight years old, then having acquired a few useful words found another ten, six of which I could have done without hearing. She still uses them! They were not picked up at home I hasten to add. We think our youngster rarely 'mimics' but this must be what happened. I suppose she saw the remarkable reaction to another child's use of them and tried herself. Certainly she soon learned how deliberately to 'place' a word to obtain maximum effect.

She knows it is wrong and interprets our frowns correctly, will stop but out it comes a few days later. Fortunately, she contents herself with the original collection and adds nothing. Many parents I know are bothered by similar events. We ignore it when it happens but look stern. When it happens when we are alone then we have a few "I don't like that" sessions. Frankly, I think there are more important things to worry about, but it can be embarrassing. It must tell us something about the success of a powerful reaction – would that people reacted to her attempts at everyday conversation in the same manner.

*Their world is different for they step to the music they hear.* Some things must be accepted about people with a mental handicap.

Much of what we call 'disturbed behaviour' or idiosyncrasies of behaviour are unchangeable parts of that child/person's personality, and they are not going to alter in any great measure. Putting pressure on them to conform only confuses and distresses them. Often they can't explain or defend themselves or protest and thus are *so* vulnerable. Much cruelty is occasioned (often by people outside the family) to them when we do not understand that they have either no control over what is happening or that it in some ways answers a need in them. I am not defending naughtiness or ill temper but we must be sure we are helping them when we judge their behaviour.

## HOLLY:

Any child with special needs has one or more qualities which make it harder for her to live in the world which mankind has created. Our society has many expectations which the disabled child often cannot meet. Yet this is the world in which our child was born, and we must help guide her in meeting the many challenges that come her way the best we can.

Our guidelines for behaviour are usually based on what we ourselves have been taught, and what we see around us. The disabled child may have a harder time conforming to these expectations because of her limitations in one area or another. It is very important that the child with special needs learns social skills and appropriate behaviour. Still, I try, with occasional success, to keep in mind where my children begin.

Naomi, at five, has just learned enough vocabulary in the past year to hold a conversation with another person. She will talk to anyone who will listen. Once the other person is engaged, however, Naomi does not want to stop, even when the other person has made it clear he is finished.

I have established various ways to let Naomi know that, although people find her very interesting, she needs to finish when they say they have to go. On the other hand, since I am aware that she does and will do this, I have learned not to be disappointed, embarrassed or mortified when it happens. If we have been invited to a social event, where I know Naomi will want to hold forth, I am aware that it will be a learning situation for both of us. If I feel I don't want to deal with that, I leave her at home. Otherwise, both of us end up feeling frustrated or angry.

I am always struck by how much the children take in from their environment. With Naomi the reaction is strong and immediate. It is more subtle with Benjamin. I have found, however, that what surrounds the children can greatly affect their behaviour. Some of this activity is beyond my control. Yet much of it, especially with small children, I can control.

For example, I can set up limits and expectations. I have found that rhythm and routine are vital in helping my children feel comfortable and confident. Rather than restricting, rhythm and routine provide a fundamental security which enables the children to act more freely. It also enables me to function in a more practical way. Mealtimes, bedtimes and nap times are the same every day. Other activities are weekly or twice weekly. Monday is grocery shopping day. Tuesday and Thursday are therapy days for Benjamin. Wednesday is reserved for errands, doctor's appointments and fund-raising for my children's medical bills. Friday is house cleaning day. These are our mornings while Naomi is at school.

Of course, we are flexible when special occasions arise. Interspersed with the main morning activity there is also room for spontaneity. Our afternoons also have their rhythmic activities. Weekends are freer, although meal and bed times are generally the same.

I made a special calendar for Naomi with drawings of the activities she can count on every day. The calendar is divided into seven days. Monday begins with a drawing of Naomi and her Papa walking to school. Underneath is a drawing of Naomi painting, followed by a drawing of Naomi baking bread. This is what happens every Monday at school. In the afternoons, I have a drawing of Naomi's bed (for rest time), followed by Naomi playing, followed by Naomi and Benjamin going to bed. The rest of the week is depicted in much the same way.

Every morning Naomi looks at her calendar so that she will know what the day holds for her. During the week, she refers to it often. Much of Naomi's more difficult behaviour comes from not understanding what is going on around her. The calendar, and our daily rhythm, helps her immensely to be able to find a reference point from which she can meet the world. It gives her a chance to anticipate with joy the coming of her favourite activities. Thus, it is easier for her to get through the more challenging ones.

Naomi's calendar

Consistency has also been a very helpful discipline for the children. The children know that when we ride in the car, Benjamin sits in his car seat and Naomi sits beside him with her seat belt on, or else the car doesn't go. There is never an exception. They know they can count on it. Both Mama and Papa say the same thing, and both Mama and Papa sit in their seats, with their seat belts on.

I have found that I must also be careful about my example. If I ask Naomi to say, "Please," I too must say, "Please". If I ask Naomi not to disturb Papa studying, she is the first to notice when I sneak into the room to retrieve some forgotten item.

Everyday I make a space to enter into the children's world of imaginative play. I make puppet shows with Naomi and I hide blocks with Benjamin. We play purely for the joy of being together. Aside from the fact that I enjoy it, that it is educational, and that it enables me to know them in a different way, it is also a way to show them that I respect their work and their needs, just as I ask them to respect mine. Even if Benjamin cannot understand this on a cognitive level, I feel he understands it deep-down. It shows in his behaviour.

I also include the children, when I can, in as many tasks as possible. We sew together, cook together and fold clothes together. When Benjamin is unable to participate physically, I talk to him about what I am doing.

I find that including as much imagination as possible is very helpful for the children to understand what I want. Rather than ask Naomi to sit still, I might ask her to pretend as if she is holding a candle in her lap, and to see if she can keep the flame from going out. Or if Naomi suddenly gets hungry in the waiting room of the doctor's office, I might pull from my pocket an invisible tea set, and she and I create a pretend tea party. In this way I try to reach my children where they are, rather than put onto them abstract ideas which make no sense to them.

There are days when nothing goes well. Other days are as if from a book. Most days are somewhere in between. The children's behaviour is not always dependent upon my behaviour, so I try not to despair when I am not handling a situation as I would like. There is always tomorrow!

Learning

# 18

## Learning

PADDY:

Learning, like so many other things is about sharing experiences with your child. Often, as the years have moved along, I have wondered who is learning the most – Sam or her parents? She has certainly helped us to explore emotions like patience, helplessness, fears, in depth as we have journeyed together. Perhaps the daily grind of teaching the same thing repeatedly, for months, has been the most difficult aspect of 'learning'. Unfortunately, we all have pre-conceptions about what constitutes learning, i.e. that it involves being still, listening, looking at books and so on but this is not how youngsters with learning difficulties profit most.

They do learn, from early babyhood onwards. They do learn but they have their own rate of progress (much like the rest of us) and it is usually slow, very slow, or almost no progress. Sometimes they appear to have stopped but mostly they start again eventually.

They firstly and most importantly have to learn the things which others apparently pick up instinctively, and so it can take parents a long time to realise where they must begin – I know that we didn't understand this for a long time. Once a way to go about these tasks is formulated, the teaching/learning stage can begin. Sam for instance, had no eye contact. After months of seeking a way through this it was suggested I blew bubbles in front of her face. For weeks nothing happened, she apparently did not see them. Then, one day, unexpect-edly, her eyes followed the stream of dancing shapes and once we had coped with our own excitement we could move on from there… to shapes, to coloured papers, fabrics, single pictures, pictures on a page, pages in a book. Then papers of different textures which when crumpled or torn made a noise and had different surfaces. Silk and wool seem unalike when fingered. Sam's little hand needed holding on them at first, but she eventually got the idea. Wool and paper offer touch contrasts, shiny smooth paper is slippery, tissue paper gets stuck in the fingers. And so the process continued.

Noise was the next thing to explore. We shook rice or marbles in a covered tin and listened. We muted the sound then by wrapping the tin in furry fabric. Next we tried water in a covered tin and we dropped uncooked macaroni on a tin tray from a height and laughed at the racket. There was a lot of mess and shouts and refusals to listen but we went on regardless but cautiously and we incidentally came to learn a powerful lesson – noise can be frightening and should be approached with care.

This way of working takes time and patience but a little each day adds up, never more than a few moments to start with and all at such a simple level. It soon develops into a time of sharing and loving. It rarely goes smoothly, for months nothing seems to happen, apparently nothing sticks in the memory or can be repeated. Somehow though, suddenly a smile of understanding breaks through and a hand reaches out to touch and it all seems worthwhile.

Sam has never stopped learning, though like most severely handicapped youngsters, there were months when she did nothing new, seemed unmotivated, listless, preoccupied with herself. Naturally we felt despair but persevered gently, avoiding too much insistence. You get to know how much they can take at a time. I always reasoned that though she was not 'actively' learning she was absorbing impressions osmosis fashion and am sure I was right.

I often think back now to the time when I quite desperately sought ways of teaching Sam the basic skills like blowing bubbles, sucking through a straw, holding things in both hands at the same time, closing eyes and hands together, hopping on one leg. It took many years to achieve these milestones.

Talking to parents of youngsters with handicaps makes one thing clear. Many (most?) of these youngsters do not play and learn in the conventional sense and so they cannot learn the lessons that building bricks offer, or play with dolls and dolls' houses. Most play needs imagination and many of these children possess none or very little. Often, at least when young, they don't mimic others or run, jump, kick things with friends. Frequently they are too frightened and prefer to be spectators. They can't be made to do these things, it simply doesn't work.

Each parent must try to find ways into this limited consciousness and appreciate the effort the youngster has to put into 'learning' – remembering to praise, and praise, and praise again and love whilst searching for the right stimulus for each one. Relish each new success, however small. Don't discount anything. One of the useful things that has occurred as a result of increasing interest in helping those with learning difficulties is the realisation that success (however limited) builds on success. When Sam was small the 'experts' tended to recognise as useful steps only significantly large leaps but things are better now. Even standing still is better than going backwards. Do be prepared for that happening too – again and again. If Johnnie seems distressed by any of his efforts then cuddling and talking makes a valuable lesson in itself. Toileting, which necessitates so much teaching and learning and is often so difficult to establish is dealt with elsewhere in this book.

These guides to learning might help:

It is not a bad idea for all parents to remember that learning starts from day one.

Cuddle and handle babies confidently talking all the time. Don't leave them out of the daytime action.

Talk to other parents and use their good ideas.

There is no need to spend a lot of money on toys. Utilise safe things from around the house. Sand and water are splendid teaching aids though everyone should wrap up well and not fuss about spills.

Blowing bubbles through clean pieces of hose of varying widths and straws etc. into clean water can help development of pre-speech sounds. Show and show, and show again.

Talk all the time to your youngster. Never mind if there are no answers or reactions, just keep talking. Exaggerate facial expressions. Concentrate on doing one thing with the youngster at a time.

And most important… be happy and make everything fun. I know it often isn't, but if you are bored it will be infectious.

People with handicaps continue to learn throughout their lives and slow though they may be they do enjoy knowing new little things providing they can absorb them in stages. Apprehension and fear are often present. Perhaps the most important thing for a parent to recognise and avoid is discouragement of yourself or your youngster. Don't be intimidated by hardened theories about play and learning. As parents of a child with handicaps we wasted far too much time with psychologists who insisted 'progress can only be achieved this way'. There are many ways. We just need to find them.

New experiences are a way of learning but what to do if the youngster does not like them? My daughter hates change of any sort. She is frightened, irritated, cries and tantrums when she encounters them. Everything must remain fixed. Furniture never move, colours never vary, static routine, mealtimes exact, car journeys always along the same routes, coffee mornings at the same restaurant. So rigid indeed is her style that one Saturday we arrived at our regular coffee bar to find our usual place occupied by a stranger. Sam walked resolutely to him and stood and stared. He tried to be nonchalant but eventually he stood up. We did explain apologetically. I hope he really understood. Madam took her rightful seat and enjoyed her drink immensely.

Sam also hates to go on holiday, a nasty word for her even though two short school trips have been successful. When we visit friends she seems to have a time span which allows her to be relaxed for a couple of hours before unease sets in. We understand these things and arrange accordingly. We explain carefully any deviation from routine knowing that she will protest. Providing it seems a useful experience for her, we insist gently that she try. When she appears to feel 'strong' we try new adventures like a picnic in a different place, a visit to a different shop or even town. Sometimes it works, sometimes not. She can, as is the way of autistic people, become difficult to handle at these times: refuses to walk and sits down immoveable, screams and cries and bites her arm. This is not naughty. She is desperately trying to let us know how hard she finds these ordeals. The world of the handicapped is circumscribed by their particular difficulties. It is tricky to decide how and when to insist on something new which will disturb the set pattern.

Sam, now twenty, is in a learning spurt; mimicking words, copying facial expressions, enjoying the trees when passing them. She'll probably stop soon, but will start again and new things will happen. I was overjoyed recently when her teacher said Sam initiated more conversation than the others. My Sam ahead of her class in something? Never! "Yes", he said, "As I was driving the mini-bus she tapped me firmly on the shoulder. "Peter Bates – beautiful trees!" Since her babyhood we have always admired trees with her, for we love to walk in woods. Something we've shared has been important. How lovely.

HOLLY:

My children at ages two and a half and five have had more formal learning than I'd ever imagined such young children would encounter. In America there are several resources for helping the young child with special needs. I found, however, it takes a great deal of time and resourcefulness to discover what is out there.

The California Regional Center provided me with the funding to enroll Benjamin in an early intervention programme. I looked at four different programmes and decided on one. Each of the programmes offered different approaches ranging from therapeutic activities in a group, to one-to-one activities with the therapist. Some met more often than others but all met at least one morning a week. Some allowed siblings – others did not. Only one group offered a support group for the parents. I highly recommend visiting at least three facilities in order to gain an overall view of what is offered, the range in quality of the programmes, and what fits best for the needs of your family and child.

It is widely recognized that early intervention programmes do make a difference to the child with special needs. The Easter Seal early intervention programme has certainly made a difference in my life. Benjamin and I attend the programme two mornings a week. During this time we see a physical therapist, occupational therapist, speech therapist and special education teacher. Each therapist spends half an hour just with us in play and gentle guidance. Talking, listening, and suggesting ways to play with Benjamin at home are also a part of each session. I have learned a great deal just by observing the therapist as she works with my child.

During our mornings there are four other families who attend. The morning begins and ends with a circle time which involves all the children, mothers and therapists. There is also a forty-five minute session for free play when the children, therapists and mothers all interact with various toys and equipment together. These times are quite special, especially as the children have grown and become "friends". One can really observe the changes in the children. During one of these play sessions, the parents join together with the social worker at Easter Seal who leads our support group. Together we share our joys, concerns and questions surrounding our special children. The social worker is also available for individual concerns and questions.

I have no doubt that the early intervention programme has helped Benjamin. I never expected that it would be such a support for me. The therapists focused on all the things Benjamin was able to do and nurtured his abilities to enable him to try for more. Each milestone he had not yet achieved was broken into small steps. Therefore his achievements were much more noticeable. Their patience, dedication and interest in Benjamin even on days when I was all but ready to quit, inspired me to re-evaluate the situation and give it one more try.

Every Thursday I participate in a sign language class given at Easter Seal. It was suggested to me by Benjamin's speech therapist when he was about one and a half years old that I use sign language in conjunction with speaking to Benjamin. It is often easier for language-delayed children to imitate gestures. It is also easier to demonstrate, guide and correct a child's outward gesture than it is to guide tongue placement and sounds. The child can visually see and participate with the therapist and parent. Many normal children make up their own signs instinctively before they begin speaking. (They will bounce up and down when they want to go out, or pat their tummy when they want to eat.) Studies have shown that learning sign language does not slow down a child's ability to speak. Rather it gives him an alternative means to communicate when speech is so difficult for him to produce. I have been using sign language with Benjamin for over a year. This past month he suddenly made the connection that if he wants a cracker, he can tell me by using a gesture. He can also more easily understand me by seeing the sign. It is a wonderful exciting revelation. Each week Benjamin is acquiring new signs and is also attempting some words to go along with the signs. Using sign language has allowed Benjmain to open a window into the rest of the world much sooner than if we had to wait for speech alone.

I feel very strongly that most influential in my children's life is their family first and their education second. All else, is icing on the cake. I therefore feel it is essential to be discriminating about the quality of education any child receives. Unfortunately we are often not given many choices for our children with special needs. Although my children have been extremely fortunate so far, I fear this will be one of the biggest challenges I will face in the future.

Naomi has been warmly welcomed into the gentle embrace of the kindergar-ten which is a part of the school where my husband teaches. Naomi is in no way an easy child to have in the classroom. Yet the love, care and time that the teachers have shown Naomi is exceptional. Because Naomi is in a classroom with normal children, Jeff and I must make a special effort to keep in close communication with her teacher. We try to carry over the same values and consistency between home and school. It is very helpful for me to visit Naomi's classroom just as it is helpful to have her teacher visit us at home. Aside from the fact that it is a thrill for Naomi, it also enables all of us to get a glimpse of how

Naomi relates to her family, her classmates, her teachers, and the natural environments in which she spends most of her time.

The other children in Naomi's class are wonderful role models for Naomi. Through the loving guidance of Naomi's teacher, the classroom children accept Naomi's differences with patience, caring and involvement. This has not always been easy due to Naomi's lack of social skills. Her teacher, however, is able to guide her constructively so that kindergarten continues to be a positive experience for both Naomi and her class. I feel it has been very important for Naomi to be in a classroom with normal children. Naomi learns best through doing and observing. What will we do for first grade? I don't know. We're taking it one year at a time.

JENNI:

Our son Daniel has been helped tremendously by the Portage Project, a method of early education for children with all sorts of developmental delay. Every week a Home Teacher visits the family, plays with the child and with the parents helps to *assess* the child's progress in each developmental area (motor skills, socialization, self-help skills, language, thinking etc.) and then week by week, choose particular home games and activities to help the child make progress in each area. These weekly 'tasks' are clearly defined and written down on a worksheet, where the parents can then record the child's success during the week. The parents receive regular support in the warmth and familiarity of their own home, and are thus considered as important team members with all the healthcare professionals. Over the months the child's progress is recorded on charts and new goals are set as the old ones are reached. Some weeks the Home Teacher spends more time listening to the parents' feelings than actually teaching the child. But this is a very significant part of the programme: thus the parents are helped, week by week, to teach their child in specific, clearly-defined ways. By strengthening the teaching role of the parents the Portage method helps the child to progress during that most crucial time from birth to school age. And the parents gain confidence that they can really *help* their child to learn.

When we began Portage with Daniel he was already 16 months old. He could not roll over, he could not sit unsupported, he gave very little social response, he rarely looked at us when we spoke to him, and he appeared not to recognize us. What he *could* do was play with toys, and his interest in toys became the key to our approach to him. Together with Glen, the Home Teacher, we carefully assessed his achievements on the Portage Activity Chart, to get a clear idea of what he actually could do in each developmental area.

Some of the first goals we set were: "Daniel will smile in response to attention by adult", "Daniel will vocalize to gain attention", "Daniel will explore objects with his mouth and learn to feed himself with his fingers", "Daniel will sit self-supported", and "Daniel will babble". From the beginning Daniel made phenomenal progress. Though we as parents were certainly experienced with parenting a child with handicaps, we were too weighted down by depression and hopelessness to see that Daniel's handicaps really were *not* the same as Marie's and that we would need to reassess our judgment of him and his potential if we were to help him to progress. The Portage method gave us the specific tools to help us do just that. No longer did I feel we were working towards unobtainable goals, for I was helped merely to work towards the next, the closest milestone, and have confidence that having reached it, the following one would be attained as well. Looking back it seems as if there was a miracle, although I know there was a lot of hard work as well. Somehow the Portage activities never seemed a burden – we just included them into our daily routines and found that they served to enrich our family life. Sometimes we just couldn't manage to do the tasks. That was all right too. Older brother Patrick often took on tasks of his own accord, and can justly be credited with the lion's share of praise for the unceasing play and stimulation he has given to Daniel. Friends and neighbours became interested in Daniel's 'tasks' and would often ask what was "on the agenda this week?" and would then play with him and help him towards his goals. A year after we first began doing Portage, a young nurse, Fiona, came to help in our family and also took on helping Daniel achieve each new goal.

Now not quite two years later Daniel appears a completely different child. Gone are all the autistic behaviours, and instead we have a bubbly, smiley, cheeky toddler. From an inert baby lying on the floor amidst his toys he has become an extremely adventuresome little lad, who has learned to stand and walk with only one hand holding on, who climbs independently up and down the stairs, up and down all the furniture, pushes a tricycle, and who plays creatively both on his own and as a part of the other children's games. Now when I survey the play room where he has been playing alone I can see the "imprint of his personality" upon the arrangement of the toys: the little cars are lined up and he has built a tower or little enclosure for them, the dollies are sitting up with the tea set carefully arranged from playing tea party, the books are strewn about where he left them after looking at them... and he is beginning to say a great many words, and clearly understands most of what we say to him. Although we know that for a three-year-old he is still significantly delayed in his milestones, we also know that he has made phenomenal strides forward, and that his rate of learning seems to be speeding up all the time.

The reader may wonder if we have had similar success with Marie. In fact, Marie was able to begin attending an excellent special school near our home shortly after our arrival in England. There she has been helped with a very similar approach and although her achievements have been more modest, due to the severity of her handicaps, she has also blossomed in the social realm and become much happier and sunnier with those around her.

The Portage method, as others similar to it, cannot change a child's basic handicaps nor provide abilities which the child does not already inherently possess. The method is perhaps not suited for all families nor all handicaps. Nevertheless it can contribute a great deal in a wide variety of family situations. And possibly its most significant contribution can be by teaching the *parents* how to strive with their child towards goals which at first may appear impossible. The method provides a framework, an understanding of early child development and specific teaching skills which can become a formidable force for growth and learning.

HELEN:

We moved to Devon partly because of the Spastics Society school in Exeter and battled with the education authorities for Keziah to be allowed to attend. She took to school very well, starting 2 days a week and now attending full time. All the staff are encouraging to the children, supportive of parents and keen to see them involved. It was most refreshing for us to meet professionals with a positive outlook. The social contact and interaction between children of her own age is something we value highly for her, and I love the fact that she now has a 'private' life and does things without either of us.

We also took Keziah to be assessed at the Peto Institute in Budapest, where Conductive Education is practised. Conductive Education, as was explained by a conductor (a group leader combining the skills of physiotherapist, speech therapist, teacher and nurse) on our first visit is "a way of life" and not simply a series of exercises. Each child has a programme of work each day using a plinth (a slatted table) and also a standing-and-sitting programme. All exercises are accompanied by song and sometimes a ball or a puppet is brought along the row by the conductor. This work enables the child, with consistent and frequent practice, to increase his or her range of movement and hopefully in time build up the movements accomplished to achieve greater independence; for example, dressing, feeding, toileting, and so on. Eating and drinking take place using the plinth as a table, and an ordinary small chair – no straps to hold wayward bodies in place. Parents have to try to give necessary physical support and are encouraged to help the children feed themselves. While this is very difficult for us with Keziah, it does feel like it gives her more dignity. It is felt by the Hungarian conductors that it is very valuable for the children to work in a group, ideally of the same level of ability and type of spasticity. Children give each other much encouragement and perhaps understand each other's difficulties and achievements more than any able-bodied person ever can.

We hosted a Hungarian conductor for a month in the summer (of 1988) who worked with Keziah and devised an individual programme for her. The enthusiasm, encouragement and constant positive feedback conductors continually give to the children is something to be wondered at. It is also infectious and very soon we too were cheering Kezzie on in her efforts to make the smallest move in the right direction. When Anna, Keziah's conductor, stayed with us, I saw clearly for the first time how much effort Keziah can put into trying to achieve something. I felt humble before such a soul who insisted on trying despite the spasms and contortions that the effort of trying creates.

Keziah is utterly distractable and this is a big problem. Her concentration is easily attracted to movement elsewhere in a room and she also has petit mal. This means she can "go off" for 10 – 30 seconds at a time. Her poor concentration on one thing makes learning difficult but it is this interest which makes her so sociable.

Keziah

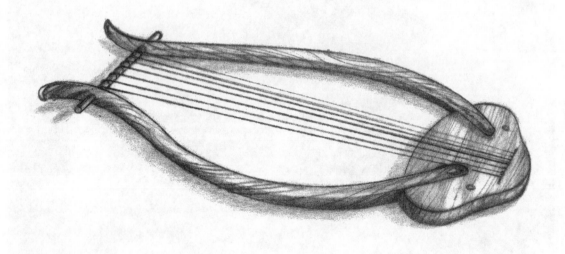

Music

# 19

# Music

PADDY:

There are two schools of thought about music in relation to people with multiple handicaps. One knows that youngsters get great enjoyment and satisfaction from music when they can join in and sing, dance or just move and relax when it is played. Others however, feel that since music is dealt with by the sub-dominant part of the brain youngsters listening become mesmerised by the beat to the exclusion of all other things.

Now, it is all right to consider music in these terms if the sounds are melodious and pleasing and perhaps can offer tranquillity or rhythms to hum or sing, and particularly if the recipient is able to decide for himself whether to have it or not.

The problem is that so much 'music' inflicted on us nowadays is brain-rot – raucous, aggressive, powerful and dominant. People with multiple handicaps are particularly vulnerable to intrusions into their life far too often because someone 'thinks that is what they want', a disguise more often for what that someone wants themselves, and even worse is the blaring noise provided just to keep them quiet. Additionally, it is expected that if they don't like the music they will just 'shut it out' but the next time they 'shut out' something they are expected to listen to, it may be misconstrued.

Sensibly chosen and used music can be enormously important in the lives of people with handicaps but it should never be overbearing in mood or decibels. For instance a guitar, recorder, lute, flute or piano when watched being played offers a much richer experience than the playing of a tape. Music should help give joy and harmony. It should be special and precious even though encountered every day. Everyone should be able to choose the music they like, respond to or need.

Joining in a melody by singing or clapping is fun. Dancing, skipping or hopping to music is too, and makes a valuable form of exercise. Some youngsters enjoy banging a drum or tambourine and it makes a good opportunity for grown-ups to join in too. Beware however, for some youngsters find this activity very alarming and should not be forced to participate. Noise, whatever its origin, is a problem area, for each person reacts differently – along the lines of one man's meat is another man's poison.

At all levels music can help to calm or be a reason to sit together and share an experience. Learning to play an instrument, even at the simplest level can be delightful for all concerned. Reciting nursery rhymes, clapping together and so finding the rhythm in the words is an important aspect of 'music' and many youngsters with speech difficulties love the repetitive fun of words strung together.

It is a crime to misuse music. Its purpose in the lives of children and adults with special needs is a rich field for exploration. It offers particular treasures in both the teaching and enrichment of each day. Its nature can change as their needs change – it serves as a wonderful meeting place but it has much value as a known friend to the solitary state.

## HOLLY:

My children have had a special attachment to music since the day they were born. They never seem to notice that my singing voice is not outstanding. Their father has a beautiful voice and we both sing to them often. We sing lullabies and nursery rhymes, and even a few old songs from the Beatles. I frequently make up songs as I go along, making them relevant to whatever we are doing. For example, yesterday when Naomi and I were cleaning, we made up a song that went something like this:

> We're dusting, we're dusting
> The table so clean.
> We're dusting, we're dusting
> The table so bright.
> We're dusting, we're dusting;
> It sparkles and glows.
> We're dusting, we're dusting;
> Oh look how it shines.

You can see the lyrics need not be deeply thought out. What is important is the joy and the relevance to what we are doing. Made-up songs are a wonderful help in getting my children through otherwise laborious tasks. Naomi can miraculously dress herself in three minutes with a made-up song. But, when I coax her or make threats, she can take half an hour.

Singing finger games and nursery rhymes gets our family through many long grocery lines, waiting periods in doctors' offices, and long car trips. Singing is wonderful, because you can take it with you wherever you go, and it doesn't take up any room!

There is a large shelf of musical instruments in our home just for the children. It has an Indian drum, a xylophone, a tambourine, a wooden recorder, harmonica, bells and castanets. I feel that it is important that the instruments be of good quality and that they have beautiful, pure tones. Our children are surrounded by enough obscure noises without giving them simulations of true sounds. Naomi and Benjamin are encouraged to handle their instruments with care and with respect. The lyre, which could easily be damaged by misuse, is kept in a special place. We bring it out only when Mama and Papa are able to play also.

Of all the children's toys, I think the musical toys are played with most often. Naomi insists upon having a sheet of music before her like Papa, whenever she plays an instrument. She even counts, one, two, three to make sure she has the right beat! We combine our music playing with puppet shows, stories, songs, dancing, or we delight in it all by itself. Benjamin's therapists have found that through music they can ignite Benjamin's interest. They have also found music to be very calming when he is out of sorts. I have found the same holds true for Naomi.

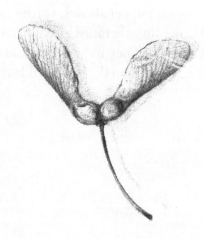

Space

# 20

## *Space*

PADDY:

We all need space. We all find it offensive if people invade our physical space or impose themselves in our mental space. People with multiple handicaps are bothered in the same way too and often more so. Autistic people especially need people to give them plenty of space, keep their distance physically, not demand replies to remarks and questions and not stare hard and long at them. It is a kindness to respect this need and makes relationships easier. Perhaps one of the greatest needs of those with handicaps is to have people understand their wish for privacy and to be allowed to make the first move or friendly overture and only when they feel ready to do so. In this way they are seen as an individual and not just one of a group. They need the compliments we can give them of seeing them as a person in their own right and not simply as someone with special needs.

HOLLY:

The world is often a bewildering place for the disabled child. Thus, the child's home takes on considerable significance. The home is a safe place, where the child feels familiar and accepted. It is a space where the child can shine.

I feel that it is especially important that our home surrounds our children with beauty, wholesomeness and warmth, and that it be a place where our children feel nurtured. One doesn't need much money, or a beautiful home in the country, to achieve this.

Our family lives in the city of San Francisco, in an apartment that is too small, and on a major street that is filled with cars, buses and fire engines. The closest green patch of grass, where the children can play, is five blocks away.

We have worked with what we have, and although we would love to have more space, less noise and an outside area of our own, we simply don't have it.

Everyone has different decorating tastes for the various rooms in their home. I feel it important to ask ourselves questions about the room we have decorated, such as the following: "What kind of mood does it project? Is it too harsh? Is it overly efficient? Is it too busy? Is it too empty? Does it generate a feeling of warmth? Is it a place where my child can sleep, play, eat or relax comfortably? Is it inviting?"

Perhaps, in some rooms, we might want to create certain moods. For instance, one might want to create a feeling of calm and peacefulness in the bedroom. For a child who is hyperactive and finds it difficult to contain himself, one might want a room that creates a protective, harmonizing atmosphere.

The colours we choose have much to do with setting the mood. Using fewer and solid colours creates the strongest mood. Think of your child napping in a room with the curtains drawn. The sun is filtering through the curtains, illuminating the cartoon football players, so that they gleam throughout the room. Alternatively, imagine that the sun's rays are pouring through a pink curtain. The room is filled with a warm pink glow. What are the different moods you have created?

Pictures can also enhance the quality of our space. The subject matter obviously conveys definite feelings to a child. What does the photograph of a race car do for a young child? What feelings does a soft water colour painting of a boy gently petting his dog bring out in a child? Pictures are not simply objects to add colour and to fill empty spaces in a room. The right picture can have a very healing effect on the child.

And how about the furniture? Is it comfortable? Is there too much of it in one room, inhibiting the child's ability to move around and play? Are there too many toys or knick-knacks around, so that the room looks cluttered? Or enough so that the room has character?

Do the children have ample and specific space to keep their toys, so that they have access to them without asking for their parent's help? Having a specific area encourages them to put their toys away when they are finished. In our home, we have set up a small play corner in the kitchen/dining area. The space has a small rug on the floor and some low shelves, which create a semi-enclosed area. On the shelves are a few simple toys – musical instruments and baskets filled with such items as stones, wooden blocks, pine cones, sea shells and coloured cloths.

It is a very cozy corner where the children can play while still being near, and a part of the centre of activity in the home.

Another wonderful addition to any household is a nature table. Ours is on a small table in the living room. Since our children are small, I do much of the arranging of the nature table. But, as they grow, I hope they will help more and more. Our nature table depicts scenes from the season, using solid-coloured cotton cloths, items from nature and a lot of imagination.

In the winter, I might create a cave using different blue and purple cloths. I might place crystals in and around the cave with, perhaps a knitted gnome or two hard at work. Pine cones and pine branches might complete the scene. In the Spring, one could use cloths in greens, yellows, pinks and blues to create a pasture with a waterfall and pond. Wooden cows and woollen sheep could graze in the pasture, while a young girl fishes in the pond. One might even add some small wooden ducks. A few green plants could be placed around for trees.

Aside from the fact that the nature table adds beauty to our home, it also involves our children in actively observing the changing seasons outside, by bringing nature inside in an imaginative and artistic way. It is especially wonderful when they can add items to the table which they have collected.

A nature table is also a lovely way to incorporate the festivals into the seasons, such as adding small pumpkins and a simple ghost to an autumn scene for Hallowe'en. This is one more way to help my children become aware of what other children might engage in out of themselves, as well as another way to pique their curiosity about the world around them.

Colour

# 21
## *Colour*

PADDY:

Colour exerts power in our life and it is easy to overlook its dominating effect on us. Think of superstitious fears about certain colours held by many, which people find difficult to acknowledge – like those who won't wear green or have it in the house. Colour choice can also persuade us we feel better than we really do when favourite colours are said to suit us. Our colour choice is a statement and from early childhood we have personal identification with selected shades because it surrounds us always and we choose or reject the colours in our rooms, clothes, luggage, make-up, garden and so on.

Colour is one of a child's earliest stimulations and it is therefore important to define its attributes to them – the how and why we respond to it. It is not enough to teach colour names, we should delve into effects like 'It makes me feel warm', 'happy', 'miserable' etc. Nor should we ignore a child's dislike of certain colours nor misinterpret their irritation over clothes or toys, putting it down to texture in a sweater or a toy's shape or noise, when actually the reaction is caused by colour or patterns. Experience shows that when parents of handicapped people meet together observations about their offspring's noticeable reactions to colours and or patterns are frequent but no one seems to have written on this important subject.

Like other children, handicapped youngsters establish very early on associations with colours, as they do with voices, sounds, and scents. Although the reaction may only be very slight or very quick it will in time turn to preference or dislike. Could it be that the colours a baby wears somehow affect its behaviour? The fashion for bright vibrant colours for babies and toddlers seems to have coincided with more aggressive behaviour in an increasing number of five year olds. Perhaps the mothers of earlier generations when choosing soft pastels for their babies' garments were responding to a soundly based instinct.

Handicapped youngsters are too often labelled 'difficult' or 'disturbed' when in reality they are desperately seeking a way to express their likes and dislikes, apprehensions and needs in the same way that others do, but speech difficulties, or limited vocabulary can prevent verbal exercising of quite reasonable reactions to daily happenings. The power of colours, the energies they exude will affect them as they do us, and their handicaps magnify these and thus may in differing and variable strengths cause them real distress.

Sam has a striped sweater she will not wear, not because she dislikes the shape or size but apparently because of the pattern which I find pleasing but she doesn't. Her bedroom, when papered in small patterns caused her to fidget constantly but she is relaxed now in a neutral soft pink which she finds inoffensive. Though not generally interested in toys she is happier with dolls and soft animals in pastel shades.

From the word 'go' Sam has rejected pictures on her bedroom walls, however carefully chosen; tearing them down repeatedly and protesting 'Don't like, Don't like'. I persevered for years to no effect then realised that she could not cope with the bombardment of colours, effects, patterns being thrown at her from the walls. After a while, when I had cleared everything away from the walls she started to choose one picture from a magazine, tear it out and carry it round with her as a most precious possession, for days and days until it wore out or was lost. Particularly prized were one inch pieces of gentle appearance which caused uproar and tantrums if mislaid. Again it took years for slow me to understand that it was the size, shade and 'feel' which made it so important (more important than toys ever were).

So the lesson I so gradually learned was to avoid colour or pattern until the youngster chose to be involved with these energies. Autistic children often find faces of figures in pictures or posters deeply threatening (Sam does to this day) and are distressed until they are removed. This is often why they won't enter a certain house or room for instance. They may however, derive great interest and pleasure from small plain coloured shapes which can be held in the hand and moved to change the colour as the light shines at different angles.

HOLLY:

We are all affected by colour – even in the most subtle ways. A bright, sunny day with clear blue skies affects us quite differently than a day full of grey clouds and darkness. We have favourite colours, colours which make us feel good. When I was a child, we used to attach colours to people in order to describe them. "She seems red because she is such a bold, dynamic, fiery person. He is deep blue because he is so philosophical and melancholy." In this way we were describing how the colours made us feel. We felt, instinctively, that colours held special qualities all of their own. Jacques Lusseyran (a man who was blinded at the age of seven) writes in his book, *And There Was Light,* that he could tell colours just by holding them in his hand.

Here is yet another avenue for healing and harmonizing. I have very consciously chosen the colours with which I have decorated my children's room. I am also conscious of the quality of colours I choose for them to wear.

When I think of colours for Benjamin, I think of joyful light colours. I want to encourage him to take hold of his little body, and be here on this earth in our family, where he is loved so much. I feel that the colours around Naomi can help encourage a peacefulness and inner strength. I take very special care that the colours are in harmony with one another for both my children. In this way I hope to encourage an inner balance.

Completely different moods can be created by the colours we choose. When one thinks of colours in this way, the possibilities for using colours as healing aids are very exciting.

Warmth

# 22

# *Warmth*

JENNI:

If we spend any time at all with little children, and especially those with handicaps, we soon see how much energy they use learning to play, to walk, to feed themselves, to express themselves. This tremendous vitality seems to flow through their activity and into the world around them. At the end of a hectic day some children still seem practically bubbling with energy while the adults around them are totally exhausted. When a young baby is learning new skills she may expend huge amounts of energy in just pulling herself up to stand, or creeping forward to reach a toy on the rug. Even more so for little children who have to overcome a handicap. They must furnish extra energy and will-power at every juncture, in order to make even the most modest steps forward.

The physicists tell us that there are indeed many different forms of energy, and the energy can transform itself, for instance, from one form to another. It makes sense, then, when thinking about the needs of the little child with handicap, to try to help her to use the energy she has to best advantage and this may mean helping her, through the way we choose to dress her, to have the most energy available for play and learning, and not to expect her to use this precious vitality to keep herself warm, or cool herself off.

Dressing a child with handicaps to give maximum comfort and energy for growing may mean that we as adults will need to look at our own attitudes towards clothing and some ideas we may have inherited about what we think is appropriate dress in various situations. Though not necessarily so with *all* children with handicaps, it can still be said that *many* of them seem to have trouble regulating their own body temperatures internally. Either they are generally cold or usually over-hot. So along with rethinking our attitudes towards children's dress, we will also need to learn to observe our own children attentively to learn what their specific individual needs are.

Sometimes parents find when they begin to observe their child that the child's evident need (say a child who often has marbled skin and extremely cold hands and feet) runs counter to their own previously unquestioned attitudes. For instance, it may be June, so the parents automatically dress the child in shorts. As parents, we can help our children best by dressing them so they will generally be comfortably warm, with warm hands and feet, yet not be so hot that they are sweating or red in the face. If we simply dress the child with the same amount of clothing we are wearing we still might go wrong, because the child's needs may be quite different from our own.

How can you tell whether a child is too warm or too cold? If she has cold hands and feet, pale skin with bluish veins showing through, reddish-blue knees, has trouble settling, seems fretful – probably she is cold and would like some extra warmth. If the child also has a heart defect or poor circulation because she hasn't learned to walk, that is even more reason to dress her with extra warmth.

On the other hand, if the child has red cheeks, seems fretful, perspires a lot, always has very warm hands and feet, his hair tends to be a bit damp with a pronounced smell to it, frequently suffers from rashes, fungus diseases or the like, the child is probably too hot and would feel better with fewer or lighter clothes.

The traditional fabrics of cotton and wool are without a doubt best for allowing the skin to 'breathe' and for the quality of covering they give to the body. If there is any tendency to over-heating, skin rashes or eczema, seek out pure cotton underwear, which is now well recognised and available for such conditions. Cotton helps to absorb perspiration, can be boiled and/or ironed to sanitize it if fungus diseases are a problem, and it seems to be non-irritating, compared with some other fibres which don't breathe, take on a static electrical charge and whose surface, after lots of wear, tends to get rough and 'knobbly'. If your child has poor circulation and tends towards feeling chilly – or indeed if she must spend considerable amounts of time lying on the floor rather than sitting, standing or moving, then wonderfully soft woollen vests and even 'long johns' are available. You'll find these in either old-fashioned, very sensible children's clothing shops, or in very new, stylish enlightened ones! They are a worthwhile investment. You can buy several sizes too big (no one notices as this is underwear) and they will last for years. They help retain your child's natural body heat, which in turn could help you retain peace of mind.

Sometimes adding a layer to the chest – for instance a sleeveless jumper, – gives just the added warmth needed. An extra pair of socks may be needed to keep little feet warm, and in winter, a child with very cold feet may benefit from a warm foot bath in the evening.

A large part of dressing a child for warmth lies in actually maintaining the warmth that has built up during moments when the child is really 'nice and cozy'. This may mean making sure that the child doesn't get chilled while getting dressed in the morning, using the toilet, or eating breakfast. It's a bit like keeping up the momentum from a downhill bicycle ride while charging up the next hill. Another moment of heat loss is the trip to school, either into the car or walking all the way. If the journey to school is by car, it is a kindness to the child to warm up the car before he or she gets into it, and of course to see that he/she is well-covered when leaving the house. Travelling outside, either in a push-chair or wheel-chair can be made a great deal warmer if the child is wrapped in a sleeping bag, zipped up, rather than just seated in the chair, even if the legs are covered, I found with my children, even when living in a very cold climate, that as long as they were inside a sleeping bag, (sometimes even with a hot water bottle at the foot!) then the air inside the bag would keep them very warm, especially the feet and legs. This way, if the little one is warmly dressed the family can get out for fresh air, even in very cold winter weather; and getting out often seems to help a lot in combating winter depression.

If the 'warmth momentum' has been lost during the day, a hot drink and a warm foot bath work very quickly to restore the temperature level. We have always seated our children on a small chair and used a plastic laundry basin for the foot baths, though for a child who cannot sit up unaided, it would be possible to set the basin on a chair at foot level, while the child sits supported in his or her normal wheel-chair or moulded seat. Gently massaging the feet and legs using a little olive oil or herbal massage oil is also a lovely way to stimulate sluggish circulation as well as transmit to the child through touch your care for him.

Another aspect of the question of warmth is the way in which physical warmth and a sense of well-being can be a means of communicating non-verbally with the child. As many little children with handicaps also haven't learned to speak it can be a great help to build up a kind of collection of ways of communicating without words, to tell our child how much we do care. If we manage to keep him or her warm and comfortable through our choices of clothing and extra effort, (and I know from experience both how hard it is to do and how easily the child can lose again the sense of warm, well-being) then the child may truly receive an on-going perception of our love, through the glow in its body. I believe this is even more important the younger the child is and/or the more profound its handicaps. Very young infants, before the age when babies normally begin to reach "gross-motor" milestones (say, up to 5-6 months, or so) can gain a great sense of security from being warm and well-wrapped in a blanket. This does not mean there are no regular play periods in the day when they are free to move their limbs and trunk and enjoy those new experiences! But it has been my observation watching a lot of babies, that those whose mothers keep them extra cozy in the first few months tend to settle and feed better, storing up a sense of well-being which helps them in later months.

Illness

# 23

## *Illness*

PADDY:

Illness is a situation which constantly complicates the lives of people with handicaps and their families. The youngster is either succumbing to something, in the throes of, or recovering from and at each stage needs extra attention. Somehow they are more vulnerable to the infections around and often it is difficult to establish 'What hurts?' or how they feel. Parents quickly become skilled at knowing the signs of approaching health problems and learn ways of taking temperatures, giving medicines, etc. without frightening the patient. One good reason for establishing early in a child's life that he knows 'teeth', throat (inside) neck (outside) etc. is so that he can show in some way where there is a problem. My daughter frequently has rashes or blotchy skin which looks awful but means little, yet she can be very ill and feel dreadful but behave stoically, so that I am never sure how serious it is. Be aware that illness is not a subject to generalise about and each youngster behaves differently and requires different handling. Sam will never go to bed, however ill, preferring to lie on a cushion or merely sit quietly in her bedroom. I accept this now but the cushion cuddled is a sign of 'poorly' times ahead.

Research is demonstrating that many youngsters with handicaps do not show the usual signs and symptoms of illness. Those with Prader-Willi syndrome for instance, apparently do not feel pain always when ill and pain is an important diagnostic aid, so those in charge should be aware of this. If you suspect something of this nature alert your Doctor to this and have him keep a note in the patient's file. Ask your doctor, too, to meet your youngster when he is not ill and observe how he looks and behaves. For a person with handicaps to meet the doctor when he isn't ill surely makes a working relationship when he is, easier.

Be aware too, that drugs apparently used without problems or side effects in the normal course of things often produce unexpected reactions in those with handicaps (particularly mental handicaps) which can be very serious indeed. Sam had a frightening reaction to a 'guaranteed safe' sedative which had precisely the opposite effect and she did not sleep for five days. Drug companies and some doctors are aware of these occurrences but regard them as numerically insignificant. It is wise therefore to use a Doctor who is sympathetic and has experience in working with people with handicaps.

A parent should not accept drugs or treatment for their youngster unless they are confident it is the right thing to do. You know your youngster better than anyone, having observed over a long period. Ask questions of your Doctor and expect reasonable, helpful answers but appreciate also that he may not have much experience in the field of handicap and may even feel helpless or embarrassed by your problems.

Try homeopathic medicine if you can. Begin by talking to a homeopath (ask for recommendations locally) to see how they approach illness. What you will find helpful is that they are prepared to give time, patience and thought to examining every aspect of a problem before suggesting remedies. Let them too, meet your youngster when he is relaxed.

Accept that illness may feature prominently in your life. Find 'backstops' who can take over shopping, or nursing or night times occasionally. Your youngster will be frightened of illness and its attendant features so spend time reassuring him that someone they love will be around all the time. Expect him to be irritable and fractious. Be cheerful and calm yourself for he will be troubled by your mood otherwise.

Do keep children home from school if you suspect an infection is on its way. This prevents spreading illness and is important because the facilities in most schools for caring for the sick are not good. A child can be quite wretched in such circumstances. Likewise, be sure the child is really fit to re-enter normal activities.

A word about dentists, for they are important. The rate of decay in the teeth of youngsters with handicaps is often faster than in others, for a variety of reasons. It is therefore important that they make regular visits to a dentist, and (if possible) brush their teeth after every meal. Finding a dentist prepared to work with people with handicaps can be a problem. Fortunately the school dental services are getting better and better. Health visitors should help mothers with children under five to find suitable dental help. My daughter needs a general anaesthetic to have even a mouth inspection prior to treatment and this is very often the case with the severely handicapped. It has to take place in hospital, necessitates an overnight stay and can be an ordeal for both of us. Hospitals, however are generally most kind and understanding, allowing the mother to stay. Actually I will not accept treatment for her unless I can stay, for it makes the whole situation easier. But I am especially careful to do what I am asked and not fuss. It has always worked well. Despite my care Sam is missing four front teeth and has many gaps elsewhere. Crowning was attempted but she broke and swallowed one. It wasn't a good idea.

Incontinence

# 24

# *Incontinence*

PADDY:

I speak as the Mother of a twenty-year-old who is incontinent much of the time, always uses pads at night and has a happy-go-lucky attitude to the whole subject! Whatever the age of your child perhaps the most helpful thing to pass on is that incontinence pads and equipment can be supplied by your health visitor, so find out what is available and keep track of improvements in this area. Since Sam was small such advances have been made and thus undoubtedly my life is now easier in this respect.

When Sam was small and not dry I used to think "Well, I don't know any incontinent adults so she must improve one day," but because she has a misshapen bladder which easily becomes infected she hasn't. She can ask for the toilet, get herself there, always remembers where it is but often needs help from then on. She is good about asking for the toilet, but leaves it late and uses a loud voice in a restaurant or just as we enter church (where there isn't one – which is why we don't go now!). Her sense of fun, I know, likes to cause a little friction occasionally and she recognised from early on the possibilities of fun here! I accept that she is not totally in control of this and never will be, though she has long spells when she can cope in daytime. I make it clear that I expect some co-operation about using the toilet and even pretend to be cross if I think she is being lazy. But when she has an infection, is stressed or ill, then she wears pads (which she puts on herself) and I don't give it any importance.

I advise that toilet training, if possible, should begin as you would for all children but without fuss or upset at failure. As early as possible establish a word which indicates the need. Praise success, take failure in your stride. Where appropriate take supplies of pads, toilet paper, soap, flannel etc. for older ones as a routine – keep some in the car always.

If your youngster shows no signs of signalling toileting needs and you think he should it may be worth discussing this with your family doctor for there may be some physical problem. The experience of my circle of parents, carers, friends, relatives of people with handicaps shows that usually the less severely handicapped do eventually become toilet trained though it takes a long time and falls apart when they are in poor health, overtired or anxious. Many of the severely handicapped, however, often do not achieve success, reliably, perhaps because they are more often ill. But many mothers stress the need for patience allied with optimism and do not let toilet training become a big issue.

If incontinence does continue, beginning school can perhaps start a regime which will help. Joining in activities with others might be a spur to conforming provided there are no physical difficulties. Often, too, teachers have ideas and ways to help home training.

If problems do continue, I believe it is wise to accept this as part of the whole, for too much emphasis is distressful to all concerned. Come to terms with the situation, find the best ways to cope (involving health visitors, etc) and leave it at that.

One last word. When I have to change and clean up Sam I make her help because I think it shouldn't become an easy option for her to be lazy. It is easier often if she lies on a towel on the floor. She must put dirty clothes in the linen basket and remember to take her bag, specially bought, with extra clothes and pads when we go out.

Holidays and travel

## 25

## *Holidays and Travel*

JENNI:

Are you thinking about a holiday with your child? Yes, it *is* possible, and yes, it *is* worth it! We take our three children across England and France every summer and have found that with adequate planning ahead of time, a few 'tricks' along the way, and plenty of goodwill we usually have enjoyed a refreshing break which has benefited everybody. Whatever your destination and however long you plan to stay, good planning will make the difference between success and 'stress overload'. We usually start planning our summer holidays during those dark January evenings. We decide on a destination (usually to visit friends or family) and begin to write letters to co-ordinate our plans with those of the people we hope to see. Then we break down the planning into several categories: transportation, funding, documents, clothes, food and in-transit-entertainment (i.e. how to keep the kids happy and quiet while we're speeding across the steppes of central France). Each of us has naturally tended to take on different aspects of holiday planning: my husband enjoys studying maps, ferry timetables, price catalogues and the like, while I enjoy planning the clothing and toys. (We tend to share the letter writing, depending upon the mood of the moment and how we feel about asking Uncle Louis if we can come for another visit after the children spilled hot chocolate on the new rug last year.) As departure day approaches, I generally do the packing while my husband loads the car. A certain amount of pre-departure bickering is to be expected at this time. ("If we're not on the road in half an hour, then we're not going!" has become a family joke.)

*Planning your destination:* Where you choose to go probably will have a lot to do with how much money you have to spend on a holiday. However exciting far away places may seem in the brochures at the travel agent's, I believe it's really what *you* make out of your holiday that counts. A trip close to home which has been well-planned, and which makes use of everything the area has to offer each family member, may be more refreshing and enjoyable than a foreign trip. We have always chosen our destinations according to how we could find inexpensive, suitable lodging, then worked out the travel details to suit. For some families camping is great fun, and transportation costs can be higher because lodging will be cheaper; for other families hotel accommodation will be necessary, so a destination closer to home might help to curb overall costs. Some families need to find a source of extra money to make a holiday possible at all. The Joseph P. Rowntree Fund, as well as other public charities, sometimes will contribute towards holiday costs! Do ask your social worker – it might be worth it! Whatever the case, I suggest starting by choosing where you would like to go. Then find the ways and means to get there.

*Plan your itinerary carefully:* Studying maps and regional guides is great fun, and it often helps by giving extra ideas about stops to make along the way or sights to see. We generally calculate mileage carefully, and choose our routes to be the *least stressful*. This sometimes means a few extra miles on the motorway to avoid town traffic, or sometimes a longer country route to make interesting, relaxing stops along the way. The important factor for us is making travelling itself as relaxing as possible. Though we generally travel together by car, the same would hold for other types of transport. We *plan easy stages,* with frequent rest stops. In the past we did try driving through the night while the children (supposedly) slept in the back, though for us it never worked well. We also generally plan our day so that we can stop for lunch somewhere where there is either something interesting to visit, a motorway restaurant with special facilities, a ferry crossing which is the right length of time, etc. In other words, we try to avoid stopping "just anywhere", because from experience we know that when the rest stops are well-organised the travel day proceeds more calmly with less undue stress. It is possible to obtain motorway maps showing where special facilities are located for disabled motorists. This can be a help in terms of access, though it doesn't always mean "full facilities". It helps to arrive at motorway rest stops just *before* the general mealtime rush. The service is noticeably friendlier then! We also plan each day's journey to end before the late afternoon, so that meal times and sleep times can be the same as at home. We try never to spend two consecutive days travelling, but plan for "rest and relaxation" days between long-distance journeys.

*When booking tickets, state your needs clearly:* If you are travelling by *plane*, contact different airlines before booking to see what they can do to help you (full accompaniment through the airport, special waiting-room arrangements, going to the head of the queue, special seating, storing of wheelchairs on the aircraft, special diets, baby facilities, etc.). I would choose an airline partly for the way its employees are instructed to cope with passengers with special needs.

It's a good idea to plan in advance for your transport to and from the airport, between terminals, and details for contingency plans if flights are not as scheduled. (We were once travelling by plane with our baby daughter who had a cleft palate, and expected to arrive at our destination in time for her next meal, which had to be puréed carefully in a blender. The plane was three hours late and we soon had a frantic baby on our hands as the airport restaurant had no food she could manage to eat, the in-flight meal was even worse, and by the time we arrived our exhausted baby had been howling and screaming non-stop for several hours. Since then we never go anywhere without food for her, prepared the way she can cope with it.) It helps when you book your tickets and state your special needs to *insist your requests be written down on your ticket*. This way every travel employee down the line will know how to meet your needs, and may even help you in ways you hadn't thought to ask about. It is important to warn airport officials at security check-points if your child is wearing metal braces or calipers because these will trigger the alarm bells.

If you are travelling by *train or coach* it helps to contact the main passenger information centre ahead of time to find out about special discounts and other help you can ask for. As train stations and bus terminals are not generally as modern as airports, you will need to plan for help with stairs, changing platforms, carrying luggage, storing push-chairs or wheel-chairs, finding special toilets, using lifts, and so on. We find time after time that a request made with a smile goes a long way in getting the extra help we need; knowing ahead of time what help we *will* need also means we try to avoid getting in the way of other passengers rushing down the platform to catch their next train. This may mean planning extra time between trains. Even if your child can walk you *still* have the right to ask for help if you need it! Some very big stations actually have special employees whose role is to assist people.

If you will be travelling by *ferry boat,* state your special access requirements when you book your ticket, when you arrive at the boat, and at every step along the line. We have found the British and French ferry employees to be extremely helpful, generally letting us drive onto the boat ahead of the other cars so that we can park by the lift. Usually the ship's nurse or other steward appears with the lift to help us carry luggage, push wheel-chairs, find suitable seating etc. On longer crossings we have always booked a cabin which helps us cope better with feeding, toileting and travel fatigue.

*Packing:* I find it helps to remember that no matter *how* well I plan, I *never* manage to get everything in, or I will find I have forgotten a crucial item and end up either making-do without it, or replacing it en route. Knowing there's no way to remember *everything* helps me to relax enough to pack reasonably logically. I usually begin, several weeks before Departure Day, by going through an entire day at home in my imagination. I write down lists of items we use at each moment of the day, under such headings as "meal times," "bath time," "dressing and bedtime," etc. Then I mentally go through all the different days of our holidays, imagining what our activities will be, what the weather will probably be like, any special occasions we'll need to dress up for, or sports we may participate in. I then make a separate list for each family member where I write down the clothes I plan to take. This helps me gradually to separate "holiday clothes" from the other ones, so that the last few days I dress the family only in clothes that will be left behind. The clothes we take serve several purposes, for example, a track suit can also be pyjamas, a sweater can serve as a dressing gown, sandals can be used for slippers, etc. It helps to take one outfit for really extreme weather, both hot and cold, as you never know when you'll get caught in a blizzard in Biarritz! Obviously it helps a lot to take clothes that are easy-care and to invest in disposable nappies, bibs and baby-wipes to cut down on laundry. It is amazing how many uses there are for kitchen paper towels!

It can be helpful to take different bags for different kinds of goods. For instance, we generally pack all our medicines and toiletries in a small vanity case (with lock) which can easily be retrieved from the back of the car if the first-aid kit is needed, without rummaging through the big clothes cases. We take a case for toys, books and "en route entertainment" items, a picnic hamper for food, and as small a bag as possible for "Kids' clothes" and "Mum 'n' Dad's clothes". (We have a family joke that goes: "Question: Where can we fit the washing machine/baby-bath/rubber dinghy/ice-cream machine/lounge chair/trampoline…? Answer: Oh, that's easy, we'll just put wheels on it and tow it behind.") Even when travelling by train or plane we have found it does help to compartmentalize. I'll never forget washing blackberry jam out of my husband's hand-knit wool Aran sweater after the jar cracked in his backpack!

*Medicines:* In the "bathroom cupboard case" we generally take: our usual medicines, all frequently or likely-to-be-used emergency medicines, a first-aid kit, and any medicines we know we won't be able to get in an emergency where we are going.

*Food:* We generally try to plan our mealtimes along with our itinerary so we can stop to eat in places with adequate facilities, and before the children have reached any extreme "hunger behaviour". To cut expenses we usually picnic, thus ensuring not only that everybody gets the food they can cope with, but also that the children's additive-free diet can be respected. We avoid soft drinks for the children and often make up our own mixture of real fruit juices, water and lemon juice. This keeps them refreshed without adding extra sugar. A bottle of water is always kept on hand.

It has sometimes been daunting for us to take our family into restaurants and motorway cafés as our children make a lot of mess while eating and people often stare at us. Frequently we have had to weigh up the advantages and disadvantages of stopping in public places which do have adapted facilities (changing tables, high-chairs, access ramps...) but where we may have to endure some shocked reactions. Sometimes we choose to eat in quiet out-door picnic areas. There we have peace and quiet, but we must be completely self-sufficient. There is no final answer. For us it often depends upon how we are feeling that day, whether we will opt for the facilities or the peace and quiet. Of course we have also had some lovely encounters with *helpful* people, like the cleaning lady who held the door open for us early one morning as we entered the café, then came up half an hour later to ask, "How are you coping, lovey?" while we were eating breakfast.

*Sight-seeing:* In addition to all the many regional guides available, a visit to the local Tourist Information Centre helps to plan sightseeing and to find out local possibilities for people with disabilities. It is hard for us to get going early in the morning, so we tend to picnic twice in one day, thus making maximum use of sight-seeing time. We try to take advantage of family-centred attractions which have interesting sights for the adults, playgrounds for the children, water and sand for the toddlers, and so on. The children have greatly enjoyed trips to botanical gardens, zoos, aquariums, beaches, forests, museums (entrance fees are often waived for people in wheelchairs), and even sitting in sidewalk cafés looking at passers-by. This past summer we were very moved to see how our children reacted to visiting gothic cathedrals. Each in their own way was visibly awed by the coloured windows, vaulted arches and flickering candles.

We try to take our children to hear live music when we can – Sunday afternoon concerts in the park, marching bands, school orchestra recitals, organ concerts in churches, and family matinée performances have all been great fun and are usually in places where the children won't bother other people if they make a little noise. In fact, by doing this we discovered that our daughter comes alive in a totally different way when listening to live music, and it seems to nourish her inwardly as few other activities do. As she now keeps very quiet we can even take her with us to evening concerts.

*Travel documents:* Along with our passports we generally keep a letter from our family doctor explaining in a few sentences our child's handicap and any relevant medication we may need. We also bring our medical record books with us, with resumé of past hospital stays, antibiotics given, allergies, weight charts, etc. In an emergency these records can tell the medical personnel clearly and concisely about our children's medical history. When we travel abroad we make sure we have extra medical insurance, and take advantage of the E.E.C. health-care reciprocity agreements by filling in a Department of Health and Social Security form before we travel. These can be obtained from large Post Offices or direct from the DHSS. It can sometimes take several months to organise our travel papers so we find we need to start getting our documents in order two or three months ahead of time, or even longer if special visas are necessary. On departure day I put our papers by the front door in a very obvious place where I won't miss seeing them. This is because on one holiday my head was so full of last-minute details that I actually *forgot* my passport at home! Fortunately we discovered my mistake only an hour after we left, but we still missed our boat anyway.

So good luck, and happy holidays!

Note: The Royal Association for Disability and Rehabilitation (RADAR) publishes annual directories on holidays for disabled people in the U.K. and abroad. These can be obtained from W. H. Smith bookshops or direct from RADAR, 25 Mortimer Street, London. WIN 8AB

Also helpful: Mobility International, 228 Borough High Street, London SEI IJX and specifically for the U.K., a Department of Transport publication *Door to*

*Door - A Guide to Transport for Disabled People* from: Freepost, Victoria Road, South Ruislip, Middlesex HA4 0NZ

Siblings

# 26

## Siblings

HELEN:

In Gloucester we decided we would like to have another child. Would it be "alright"? Keziah's cerebral palsy was of unknown origin. We decided against the (few) tests that were available and asked the higher powers to order our lives in accordance with our capabilities. We made one decision, however; given two spastic children, our family would be big enough!

As Keziah is so sociable, we felt that having siblings would benefit her, and us, and I'm sure that it was the right decision to take. We were conscious too that having a sibling would mean Keziah had less individual attention and might not progress physically so well, without so much intensive help. Guilt can show its face here and parents have to face such questions when deciding to have a family around the nucleus of a first-born.

Fred came in early July, just before Keziah's third birthday. Trevor's course finished a few weeks later, and we moved to Devon in September. It was a time of many changes. But Keziah showed no sign of envy at her new brother; she loves any attention he shows her now even if this entails him climbing on top of her while she is on the floor and being his "horse", or his attempts to do "physiotherapy" with her.

Of course we wonder what it is like for Fred to have a sister like Keziah. We try not to make him feel too responsible and "grown up" too early. There seems little fear of this! One thing I think is hard for him comes from Keziah being at school full-time. Every weekday, during school hours, it is as if he were an only child, but for the rest of the time he has to learn to make the space for Keziah and her special needs. Very often Fred uses the opportunity of Keziah having all of someone's attention to create a diversion to himself. Now this is entirely natural but complicated by the fact that Keziah is completely dependent on her carer for physical stability and it's not so easy quickly to leave her to rescue the cat, remove the bread knife, or whatever. Tempers often rise although we try to encourage patience.

We have now come to the point of deciding to have a third child and indeed I am newly pregnant. Again we stand on the threshold of change and new questions, new problems and new solutions are all waiting to present themselves. Also the old questions: how much time can we afford to spend on other children when Keziah has such great need of us? Where will be the time to practise her programme of Conductive Education at home?

My answer to these fearful questions comes with the feeling of rightness of Keziah being part of a family. Her siblings will know her above all else as their sister and hopefully will always have a special place for her in their hearts. Maybe too, it will positively affect their attitudes to disability generally as they mature and become adults. Something in me encourages my wishes for more children and says that Keziah will benefit from having lots of life around her, in the shape of siblings. This faith allows me to enter the situation of having Keziah and two small children to care for, knowing that it will be physically difficult and emotionally tiring, but also hoping that it will be possible and will somehow work.

DOUG:

Doug Sim writes as someone who grew up as the "normal" sibling of a handicapped sister, and how this affected his life. He remembers an English, post-war childhood:

Soon after I was six, when my older sister was eight and my brother was two, I remember the excitement in our home waiting for Mother to come home from hospital with our new baby sister. When baby Ruth eventually arrived, she really was beautiful, with dark hair and lovely eyes, which were to become almost black. At the time we didn't know about the trauma which Mother and Ruth had gone through. A complex and clumsy delivery resulted in Ruth being starved of oxygen and receiving brain damage. The consequence, complicated by jaundice and separation from her mother, was that Ruth began to have mild convulsions, was very tense and tearful, and couldn't sleep. Then Ruth did not develop normally: she neither learned to sit nor crawl, and although she could react with the full range of emotions, she never learned to speak.

For the next five years, Mother and Father worked ceaselessly to find help for Ruth. This was during the immediate post-war period, with all the shortages, deprivations and prejudices. Medical caution, indifference and ignorance abounded. Though skilled and dedicated amateurs offered limited help, professional help was almost non-existent. Despite these endless problems and fruitless visits to specialists, family life continued happily, and our special sister was the joyful centre of all our attention and affection.

My happiest memories are of family picnics, long walks and visits, when Ruth loved being pushed, especially at a run. Her favourite game was being pushed up a steep slope, to rush back, gathering speed, towards the waiting, well-braced catcher at the bottom. I cannot recall *ever* feeling neglected in any way, although Ruth needed constant care. We naturally included her in all we did, whether a birthday party, cricket in the road, or bath-time, with me at the "taps end" holding Ruth, and younger brother at the "sloshing end", all three joining in with splashes and bubble blowing. Our move to a bigger council house provided us with a long, gently-sloping, newly-paved hill, which was the perfect highway for our recently completed soap-box trolley. It had an enclosed rear passenger seat where Ruth could sit, wedged in with cushions against the inevitable buffets, and wrapped in blankets against the keen Kentish air. Neighbours frowned their disapproval at such recklessness, but Ruth happily bumped to a halt on waste ground at the end of each rapid run. One notable winter I held her on my lap on my trusty sledge as we made the same descent, Ruth screeching with delight. Such normal behaviour was the hallmark of our family and came decades before the current, long-overdue trend towards "normalization".

Then my parents read a magazine article about a special school in Aberdeen founded by Drs Thomas Weiss and Karl König. Ruth was taken to see Dr König in London. He gave our family the first hope of specialised care, and advised that my parents press the local authority to support special schooling for Ruth at Camphill House in Aberdeen. An official came to visit us and agreed to recommend that Ruth be sent to Scotland. When she eventually went when she was five, the wrench and sense of our loss was enormous, especially as Aberdeen was so far away. However, within a year, exciting news arrived: Ruth, along with five other children who were suffering from the rigours of the Scottish winter, had been chosen to form the nucleus of a new Camphill school at

Thornbury, in Gloucestershire.

By February of the following year, our family had packed everything into a van and moved into the hurriedly-converted back room of the stables at Thornbury Park. For me, at 13, it was a wonderful change. I loved the atmosphere of the big mansion house, as well as meeting so many new members of the community, many of whom were not English, which was a new experience for me. And I could again be with my sister, and now, too, with her delightful companions. It was a cheerful, pioneering time for all.

At this point, I began consciously to realize all the many benefits that Ruth was bringing to my life. Our own family was united, I was enjoying the pleasures of life in a wider community whose members all worked towards the same central aims. It was a cultured, artistic milieu, which helped me to gain further love for, and belief in, those people with handicaps, which so many sections of society prefer not to acknowledge as persons in their own right. Also, my change of secondary school at that time was to have a profound effect on my life, for there, on the first day, I met and fell in love with the girl I was to marry. In that school I also found my vocation for teaching woodwork, which I have done since leaving training college.

So the sister with whom I have always most closely related brought me towards the most worthwhile and valued aspects of my life. Although much of the credit for my upbringing goes to my parents, Ruth was the catalyst in the major events of my life.

Respite

# 27

## *Respite*

HOLLY:

The emotional and physical demands on the mother of a child with special needs are overwhelming. Even jobs demanding one-tenth the output, offer lunch hours and coffee breaks. The special parent, especially if she stays at home with the children, often gets none. Not only that, she is on call twenty-four hours, seven days a week. No one can function optimally under such conditions. Respite is essential.

It is sometimes hard to find people who are qualified to take care of a child with special needs, while the mother takes a break. Regular baby-sitters are often unacceptable because they haven't the knowledge or confidence to take care of disabled children.

In America, there are agencies which provide respite for parents of disabled children, but very often families do not meet the strict criteria required in order to get the funds to pay for it. A couple of my friends put up notices in the special education or nursing departments of local colleges, requesting help from students. Another friend trained her regular babysitter in the special care which was needed to look after her disabled child.

I have a reliable babysitter who comes regularly one afternoon each week. I find that keeping a rhythm is most helpful for the children. They know when the babysitter is coming, and they know that Mama will return soon; I always do. As a result, I have an afternoon during which I can meet with a friend for coffee, see a doctor, get my hair cut, or go to the library. Of course, I often use the time for errands, too, which would otherwise be impossible (or at least problematic) if I took along my two little cherubs. I am always refreshed. Not only do I accomplish things, but the time alone allows me to gain perspective on my children, on me, my feelings and my thoughts.

Nap-time is often an additional respite-time for me. This does not replace getting out of the house, but it is nurturing. Although Naomi, at five, does not usually sleep in the middle of the day anymore, she has a quiet hour in her room while Benjamin takes his nap. It is easy for me, at this time, to do household chores. However, at least three or four times a week, I use this hour just for me – to read or to write. If we mothers, whose children are an extraordinary challenge, are to find the strength to meet the challenge, then respite is a must.

## PADDY:

It makes sense that to do any task well will mean wise pacing and regular breaks. Care of handicapped youngsters often includes daily arduous or boring routines and physical tasks which sap both the energy and spirit of the carer. It often means learning patience and how to endure boredom and frustration and it includes knowing that progress will be slow often to the point of stopping. Every parent needs and has a right to come up for air – preferably on a regular basis, so take every chance you can.

Holidays away from home necessitate finding alternative care for the youngsters and frequently this is almost impossible to achieve. Parents have to work at this problem and establish ways that mean they may get away, even if it is just for one day.

Just as important for each parent, is to cultivate interests and hobbies which give them escape from the day-to-day slog and provide something to look forward to. There is sense in making a few hours each day or every so often to read or listen to music, take a walk, visit the theatre, or meet friends. There is no reason to feel guilty about this for if the situation is not lightened sometimes then 'Mum' becomes tired and dispirited through tiredness and misery.

Associated with this are also the doubts many parents (particularly mothers) feel about their child going away from home for a 'stay' somewhere. Naturally every parent will want to feel satisfied that their child will be properly and lovingly cared for at these times – that is the first essential – but then it is easy to worry that the handicapped youngster may sense rejection or encounter unhappy experiences. I have suffered my own mixed emotions about this subject but acknowledge it essential that a handicapped person, and however severely so, should try to establish a little independence though it may take a very long time and not be without some heartache on the part of parents. Providing positive steps are taken about the whole issue, the right for instance to reject respite care which doesn't meet good standards (and understanding that the nature of parenting and caring for those with handicaps means "little doubts" may persist), then a break on both sides can do much good by offering new experiences.

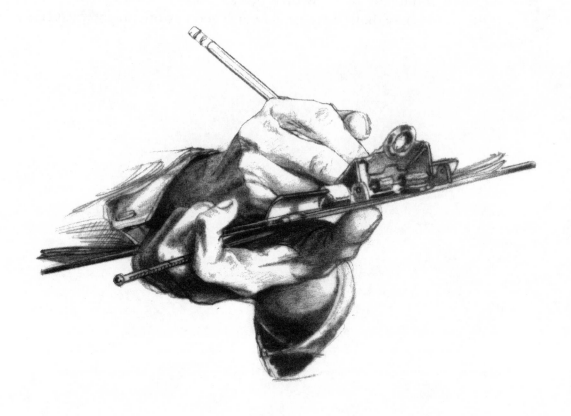

Professionals

# 28

## *Professionals*

*The doctor assists, but Nature heals*

Paracelsus

HOLLY:

I have seen a variety of specialists in relation to my children's delayed development. I began this long medical search hoping to find answers. When answers did not come, I wanted a label that would make my children financially eligible for the therapies I was told they needed. The doctors sympathized with my plight, but said they could not help.

Most of the doctors I encountered exhibited interest and concern for our family. Yet I always came away with the feeling of great distance between us. Although they made their living working with parents like me, I felt they had no idea what it was like to be the parent of a child with special needs. They showed great interest in the facts and the data regarding my children, yet I had the feeling they were only taking into account the shell of my children. My children are so much more. Many of my observations were tossed aside when they did not fit into what the doctor felt was important.

The doctor is the professional in his field. He knows all about various medical abnormalities, what their causes are and what can or can't cure them. He knows this from his studies, his medical texts and from his experiences. He deals with scientific facts, which he puts together to form diagnoses and prognoses for children every day.

I, on the other hand, am in a sense the best expert on my child. No one knows his needs, his habits, his movements, his behaviour as I do. The knowledge I have of my child is a constantly living, forming, growing one. The doctor draws on that knowledge, asking many questions, giving me forms to fill out, translating that knowledge into facts to form a diagnosis. Facts that often reduce my baby to a scientific statistic.

And then, of course, there is my child. It always strikes me as very strange that the doctors spend 85% of their time talking to me, reading my child's medical files, and only 15% of their time actually in contact with my child. And what does the doctor do with my child? He measures him, and pokes him and gives him old, broken plastic toys to play with in his white, sterile office. Does the doctor really think he can get an accurate view of my child in this way? Or doesn't it matter?

And then I ask myself, what does the doctor really see? If he disregards a true observation of my child, and tosses aside the living insights I have to offer, with what is he left? He is left purely with the facts he chooses to make important, based on his scientific knowledge. The doctor is very limited.

Recently, my husband and I were very fortunate to be able to take our children to see two Anthroposophical doctors in Europe; in addition to the usual medical training, these doctors have studied Anthroposophical medicine. The first doctor spent her entire morning with our family. She gave us juice and cookies. She took us for a walk. She talked with my husband and me at length. She brought out a box of toys and played with the children. She talked with the children. She laughed with the children. And all the while she observed the children.

The second doctor spent an afternoon with us. He, too, observed and played with the children in a way no other doctor had ever done before. The quality woollen toys and the warm and inviting way in which both offices were decorated were noticeable statements of the care these doctors feel for their patients.

Jeff and I felt both doctors were truly involved in exploring each aspect of our unique children. They treated our children with joy, with respect and with dignity. We felt that the valuable insights and suggestions they gave were based on truly experiencing our children. In "mainstream" medicine this approach has genuine constraints: pressures of time and money, sheer numbers of patients, and problems of organization. This is understandable. But if individuals felt inspired to make even small beginnings in their own corners of the conventional medical world, this would have its own impact. Meanwhile, parents will always appreciate and remember the professional who genuinely relates to the child.

HELEN:

Diagnosis of Keziah's problem came slowly. My partner, Trevor, and I were blissfully unaware of "normal" child development and enjoyed having a young baby to love and care for. This time was a period of grace. We were able to walk in the hills, to spend time on a beautiful beach nearby, to visit friends, all the time oblivious to the special difficulties of the person we were now nurturing.

In time relatives murmured, and commented, and asked vague questions. Eventually we visited an on-the-ward clinic attended by a paediatrician. We went a number of times before he was able to give us a diagnosis. One day the paediatrician came with a number of medical students, to the corner where the three of us were waiting. Holding Keziah up under her arms, he said, to the students "This is Keziah and she has cerebral palsy". We were dumb-founded as it was the first time he had ever made a definite diagnosis. We immediately questioned him and were brushed aside with offhand and somewhat annoyed assurances that of course we'd been told before. Not for the first time, I came away from the clinic in tears, not of sadness at Keziah's condition but with anger and frustration at the way we had been treated.

JENNI:

When we, as parents, are in a state of hurt and uncertainty, then it registers terribly deeply if medical situations are handled ineptly or inadequately. We hear so much that is negative – "he'll never do this", etc. When Marie was 14 months old, she still could not sit, hold an object, eat from a spoon, or focus her eyes. We were visiting my family in California. My sister dragged us 200 miles to visit an early intervention centre for infants with developmental delays. We spent the morning in the centre, on a warm rug, surrounded by toys and friendly people. The psychologist said: "Look, Marie is trying to grasp the bell". (To us she just appeared to be scratching her fingers on the mat.) The teacher for visual handicap said: "Look, Marie is turning her head towards the side where the bell is." (To us she *wasn't* focussing her *eyes,* so we didn't notice the turning of the head.) In that morning these kind people gave us back our daughter with new possibilities. They taught us to look at what she *was* doing and not at what she *wasn't* doing. They had helped us to see our daughter beyond her handicaps. They told us all about the programmes for babies at their centre. They gave us armloads of books, parents' magazines, scholarly articles. They gave us a sense of the dignity of people with handicaps and the courage to be our daughter's advocate.

PADDY:

Generally speaking, you will save yourself a great deal of tension and disappointment if you do not expect too much, too fast, from professionals. Experts are encountered in the fields of social services, education, health, etc. but they operate under financial restrictions thus frequently having to make difficult decisions as a result. They are often short staffed, inadequately trained and have to combine care of people with handicaps with other disadvantaged groups. Whilst some can appear unsympathetic most do want to help.

Parents will find they get a better response if *they* establish a good working relationship with professionals. Ask questions when there is a problem and don't be shy of explaining your need for help. A telephone call to a health visitor or social worker can set your mind at rest but if you wait to be approached you may wait a long time. So make yourself known.

Once your child is at school not only will professional people deal with aspects of education but they will point enquiries in the right direction of dental care, physiotherapy, etc. and frequently act as a general advice centre. Get to know all the teachers at school and seek out introductions to their sources of expertise.

If you are unhappy with the professional care available to you and would like alternatives, talk with other parents, social workers (you can approach one not your own if you wish), local council members, etc. All sorts of help is available but the onus, unfortunately is on you to seek it out.

It is worth remembering that associations exist to help parents/carers of people with handicaps and it is worth joining them for their general help particularly as subscriptions are usually low. Do not wait until you are in despair before looking for advice but use times when pressures on you are less than usual to find out what exists in your area and keep written notes and telephone numbers. Above all remember that other parents have a fund of practical experience – so dip into that. Parents are professionals, too.

Friends who are doctors, nurses, teachers are useful as ideas bouncing boards when a problem needs talking through. A lot of difficulties can be resolved by discussion with someone who will listen. A sensible, kindly person in this capacity is often more valuable than an 'expert' with formal training but little real 'hands-on' experience.

One last word, professionals I know feel vulnerable too and appreciate gratitude for their help. Sometimes we tend to think we have a right to everything and most professionals are human too.

How to get help

*29*

## *How To Get Help*

HOLLY:

Once I established the fact the my children needed help, the long struggle to find it began. The first thing I did was to seek independent medical evaluators. The neurologist I saw suggested a special nursery school programme for Naomi. I found that these programmes were far beyond our means. I then turned to the public school system where Naomi was tested and qualified for a special education class. I visited the class and knew immediately that it was all wrong for Naomi.

Meantime, I realized Benjamin, too, needed help. During my visit to a school for Naomi, I inquired where I might go for help for Benjamin. A temporary home-based infant programme, where the therapist would come to our home weekly, was suggested. Soon after, I enrolled Benjamin in the Easter Seal programme, where he now sees four therapists a week. I eventually enrolled Naomi in a very special private nursery school and obtained speech and occupational therapy for her through the public school and privately. I also found a support group for myself.

Because of our limited American medical insurance, and the fact that my children do not have a diagnosis that fits into an acceptable category, we rarely qualify for financial coverage from our insurance company. I, therefore, have spent many hours on the phone, and many hours writing letters, in order to find the funds to cover my children's medical and therapy bills, which amount to hundreds of dollars per week. By now, it is easier because I have made my contacts. Still, I must constantly keep on top of it in order for much of the therapy to continue. The following are the guidelines I have used to get the help I need:

*Begin:* Make a phone call, talk to a friend or thumb through the phone book around the headings "Disabled", "Handicapped", or your child's specific disability. When the person you talk to cannot help, he or she will often refer you elsewhere.

*Be Specific:* Once you establish what you are looking for, describe it as best you can. That way you are more likely to get what you want. If you haven't established what you are looking for, do some research. Go to the library. If you feel comfortable talking it over with a friend, do it. The friend may have a friend, or know of an organization that can help.

*Have Patience:* The person you want to talk to is often not there. Leave your name and number, but don't wait for them to return your call. Find out when they will be in, and you call them.

Often, you have found what you want by now. If not, don't give up.

*Be Persistent:* I once called three times a day for two weeks before Ms X accepted my call. Even then, she put me on hold for one-half hour.

*Be Calm, Clear and Courteous:* This is not always easy, but it does help. People are much more willing to listen to you if they feel they are not under attack.

*Go to the Top:* If you feel you are getting nowhere with the person to whom you are speaking, ask to speak to his or her immediate supervisor, and on up to the top, if necessary.

*Keep Records:* Keep records of those with whom you have spoken. When you need to go to the top, give that person the names of the people you spoke to previously and the approximate dates. This will attest to the time and effort you have made to find a solution.

*Appeal:* If you have reached the top and your request is turned down, write a letter of appeal. Put in writing what you want, what you have done so far to get it, and why a rejection is not acceptable to you. Keep the letter as clear and as concise as possible, again using names and dates to verify your efforts.

These are the steps I use (and they have been effective) to get the help I need for my children. Good luck!

JENNI:

One of the most difficult aspects of caring for our children in infancy was feeling alone and not knowing where to turn for help. Sometimes we had only a simple question we wanted to ask about baby-care or minor illness. Several times we were faced with an emergency and we needed immediate medical help.

We were struggling to re-organise our way of life to accommodate the changes brought by our children's handicaps, and we needed financial help to pay for equipment, child-care, medical appliances and complementary medical treatment. We also needed help to set up a home-based educational programme to encourage our children's development during the pre-school years. Gradually we began to sort out the different areas in which we needed help, and where to look to find it. Generally speaking, as parents *we are our own best helpers*. When we know what we want, and put enough energy into getting it, we will usually meet with at least some measure of success. From my experience, I would say: don't expect anyone else, no matter what their title, to do it all for you.

If you need *medical* help, start by contacting your family Doctor, Health Visitor, District Nurse or Specialist Health Visitor for Handicap. If you feel your child needs to be seen by a specialist, then either get a referral from your G.P., or, failing that, from any other doctor with whom you may have a good contact. If that doesn't work, then try making an appointment directly with the specialist in question. *Persistence pays*. It once took me nine months and several doctor's visits to get an appointment for my son to attend a hearing clinic. When we finally got to the clinic my intuition that the boy was suffering a significant hearing loss was confirmed by tests. If you are not happy with the doctor's opinion, go to another doctor. This is called "obtaining a second opinion". *Remember, your intuition about your child is probably right.* If you feel your child needs emergency medical care, and you can't reach your doctor, don't hesitate to take the child to the hospital. This is particularly true in infancy, when very serious illness can develop rapidly, and as parents you may be the only persons tuned into your child enough to pick up the danger signals.

If you need practical or financial help, I suggest the first step is to get a social worker. In Britain this may mean some clever sleuthing on your part, but by ringing Social Services, (in the business phone book under the name of your county), you will be able to get the name of the social worker who is responsible for your geographical area. The next step is to actually get her on the phone to make an appointment to see her. This may take a lot of persistence, but I have found that by ringing very early in the day, just after the office opens, I generally get through to *someone* who can help. (Don't ring just before lunch or late Friday afternoon!) By ringing back every day until I get my social worker, I have managed to get an appointment in the end. If you "keep a smile in your voice," the secretaries will soon get to know you. This is useful because secretaries often carry a lot of responsibility, and can get things moving, if they are on your side.

Don't depend on telephone messages being delivered, or having calls returned; though sometimes this *does* happen, regard it as a nice surprise. It helps to remember that social workers are extremely busy people, and by being persistent and clear about your needs, you can actually help them, because they know you are a reliable "partner" in getting the help you need. When you've got your social worker on the line, don't settle for vague promises, such as, "Oh, I'll try to call in sometime next week." Insist on an exact time and place, agreeing beforehand what information or forms the social worker will bring, and any preparation you are to do for the meeting (such as finding medical records, official documents, rent receipts, pay-slips or the like). The Department of Health and Social Security prints a number of booklets, obtainable at all larger post offices, on the benefits and income supplements available to families who have a handicapped child. We found it helped to read the booklets and fill out the forms *before* our social worker's visit. As it turned out, she needed to check new legislation and we might have missed some benefits if we had depended on her initial information. Once the forms have been filled out and sent to the appropriate offices, *don't forget about them*. Keep chasing them up regularly, even making long-distance 'phone calls to central offices if necessary, until the benefits come through. It took us nearly a year to get one benefit, but when it finally was awarded, it added one fifth extra to our monthly income!

Your social worker should also be able to help you get home-help, respite care through the Handi-care scheme, grants to remodel your home (for such things as installing a downstairs bathroom, central heating, ramps, etc.) and help in replacing important home appliances i.e. washing machine and clothes dryer. The social worker or health visitor can help you obtain free nappies and other incontinence supplies for your children when they reach the age when they would normally be out of nappies. It is also possible to receive small grants to help towards the cost of a family holiday. And finally, your social worker would know of various charities who could be approached for help towards specific items, treatments or equipment.

If you are looking for *moral support*, I highly recommend joining a local parents' group relating to your child's specific handicap; Mencap, Contact-a-Family, the Down's Children's Association, the Spastics Society, ASBAH (Association for Spina Bifida and Hydrocephalus), the Cleft Palate Association, are only a few of the many groups which exist. A list of some of these parent groups is at the end of the book. If you need help finding an address or group in your area, I suggest consulting: the telephone book, the librarian at your local library, your town Citizen's Advice Bureau, or local clergy-person. Often small-town newspapers produce an annual directory of local services which can be obtained by ringing the newspaper. The person at the information desk of the nearest hospital can sometimes help locate self-help groups related to particular illnesses, which may even meet within the precincts of the hospital. And of course the Samaritans are always there to help, and they may be able to refer you to the organization you are looking for.

If you need help – either physical, moral or financial – for a *very big* cause, such as raising the money to take your child to a treatment centre abroad, finding volunteers to help you with intensive therapy in the home, or funds to pay for important surgery or similar urgent goals, it may help to approach several service groups for sponsorship.

Organizations such as the Rotary Club, Lions Club, Kiwanis, and Scouts have, as part of their reason for being, the goal to help people in need. If you also contact your local newspapers and radio stations, you may find they have a person in charge of human interest stories who would be willing to write an article about your child and the goals you are trying to reach. This publicity can sometimes attract a lot of support, helping to reach goals that seemed impossible before. I know a mother of a very large family who wanted to raise money for the special infant centre where her son who had severe handicaps, was receiving important treatment. The centre had been threatened by a loss of funding and its very existence was in jeopardy. So the mother did a sponsored 300 mile walk from Torquay to Gloucester. The event was well-covered by the local press and she raised a huge amount of money for the centre!

For any further questions, I suggest getting a copy of the *Disability Rights Handbook*, published yearly by The Disability Alliance ERA, 25 Denmark Street, London WC2H 8NJ. (Telephone: 01-240 0806.) This handbook gives clear and thorough descriptions of all benefits available in the U.K. It also presents the exhaustive list of parents associations, research organisations, trust funds and advisory groups for every handicap or disease imaginable.

In the U.S.A., contact the National Center for Education in Maternal and Child Health, 38th and R Street N.W., Washington, D.C. Telephone: (202) 625-8400.

New dimensions

# 30

## New Dimensions

PADDY:

It is easy, as one grows along with a person with handicaps, particularly those with severe retardation, to forget that although their mental age may be low, perhaps functioning at only three or four years, physically they get older. It has to be understood that they are not just a little chap in a big body. Parents and carers of these youngsters are often surprised to run up against behaviour problems that are in effect teenage rebellions – sulks, tantrums, irritations, waywardness and so on. Somehow the hormone system evolves and they start to act like the teenagers they physically are and so begin to feel frustrated, hampered by speech difficulties, physical problems, lack of mobility and so on. The ages of fifteen or thereabouts to over twenty can be a most taxing time for parents and carers as they see these changes occur and experience the backlash.

There are no certain ways to approach these stages. Patience is undoubtedly necessary. Understanding and love too. Calmness is the only way to deal with outbursts for they can be violent and thus upsetting for others around. Often parents have said that it took quite a while, when this hitherto unknown 'disturbed' (and disturbing) behaviour surfaced to realise what was happening. Parents of 'normal' teenagers know all about these years! Somehow it makes it easier to endure and handle well when put in perspective. As a stage it does pass but it can be difficult and distressing for all involved particularly when it coincides with finishing at school and moving onto other things. Perhaps the worst part for parents and carers is getting through to the youngster that they do understand, sympathise and above all, care.

## A Kind of Adolescence

*Does she think we don't listen?*

*'I hate you', 'hate you', 'hate you'.*
*Words that come over so clearly.*
*Words that I have never imagined to hear.*
*Words that I hoped never to hear.*
*But 'I hate you' rings out.*
*Frenzy, frustration,*
*Anger, angst,*
*Pain, misery,*
*Fear.*
*Her face puckered in fury*
*She bites at her wrist,*
*Then screams, then hurls a chair,*
*The china doll follows*
*Then book, paper, pens and pencils from the desk.*
*She runs in torment throughout the house*
*Sobbing rage, desperate despair.*

*We follow only to protect her.*
*Mute for no words help.*
*Kicks and lashings.*
*We say 'We are here. We care'*
*Helplessness sees torment.*
*Sadness views nightmare.*
*Peace be with you both say I.*
*The air electric stills a little.*
*Are we going into calmer waters?*
*I pray to take the right course.*
*She can express so little in words*
*And cannot say 'I hate you'*
*But can only act it.*

After twenty years with my daughter I offer these qualities as the most helpful in avoiding disorientation by such problems... calmness, sensitivity, a philosophical acceptance of whatever problem currently confronts you and an always enquiring mind.

I am mindful of Keats' dictum:
> *As with us mortal men, the laden heart*
> *Is persecuted more, and fever'd more.*      *Hyperion* Book II. 101

For it does seem that having a handicapped child means experiencing extra hurts – maybe family or friends who never consider offering help because you manage everything so efficiently anyway, or never imagine how awful it is to ask assistance (which is why most parents don't of course!) or of being embarrassed by the transparently untruthful, quickly thought-up excuse. So many would be willing to help if only... they had the time or were not going out that night. And naturally, there is a great fund of advice on how you could do it all rather better – not unfortunately based on coal-face experience.

If only it were possible to teach other children to appreciate that just because a youngster with a handicap doesn't reply immediately it isn't because they aren't delighted and excited by the friendly approach and even more about the hurt and rejection they suffer when they run towards the swings and the other kids disappear.

It is especially searing to listen to a conversation dominated by talk of other youngsters or teenagers – their excellence, cleverness, and career progress. A wise woman can comfort herself with the unexpressed thoughts that her child's apparently small but actually very considerable strivings (to move or speak a little) are on a par with the more obvious 'normal' achievements. It is too easy to overlook that within a damaged body is an extremely courageous person trying to overcome real shackles. It is saddening too, for your child to be regarded as an object of pity and not as a person. Strange how being presented with the problems of the handicapped "face to face" bring out oddly unpleasant attitudes in some people – witness for instance the struggles associated with trying to establish small community homes.

However, all that it needs is courage and consolations of real value and this is where the 'older' parent wins. I use Keats' comment about a heart too burdened for too long becoming hard and stony to remind myself to take positive steps about helping myself to retain an interest in, an amusement about and a concern for my immediate and the far-flung world. It is easy to become self-centered: worth working at to remain open hearted and ever compassionate. Others face immensely difficult lives, too.

So, I've learned that I help myself when I accept my life as a task like any other – to love myself as well as my child. If this means allowing myself the occasional complaint or tear, well – so be it. But I laugh a lot and enjoy the small treasures in life as a balance where ever possible even if it means leaving the dishes unwashed for a while! It is wise also, to avoid being too hard on yourself when you appear (to yourself) to be over sensitive about others' attitudes to problems such as yours. It is natural to feel deeply. When you are reacting to vicissitudes and still have a sense of purpose the heart is far from stony and sinking into apathy must be dreadful. Even the anguish of despair can be used positively. If you don't expect too much of human nature you won't be hurt and indeed may be (as I am so often) deeply touched by some unexpected kindness to yourself or your child.

Coming of age and letting go

# 31

# *Coming of Age and Letting Go*

PADDY:

All children have to leave home some time and this includes youngsters/adults with handicaps. Parents will be aware from the start that one day they will be too old or too ill to continue to care for their offspring. People ask the question "What's going to happen then?" even when these children are babies and will then suggest that it is kind or sensible to prepare the child for the inevitable break, when they are young. In theory, sensibly, this is so. Working it out however, may be well nigh impossible.

The central difficulty is that many authorities do not offer respite care or think to the future of those who will not be able to lead an independent life after they are sixteen. As a result therefore, a child or teenager does not get used to being away from the family for say, a weekend a month which would be a sensible way to begin to establish some independence. When this care is available carers should take the opportunity to have a rest and see it positively as a chance for their youngster to launch out on his own a little bit.

Sometimes care which is offered proves to be unsuitable and parents should not hesitate to stop visits if they feel all is not well with the situation. Instinct is important. Additionally, some youngsters, like those with autism for instance, become enormously distressed by changes in their environment. Then parents will need to decide the worth of breaks for their child away from the security of the family, particularly when recovery from these episodes takes a very long time. Nobody can make this decision but those nearest the child.

How to handle all these problems and the difficulties that come in their wake do worry parents as do many decisions about the welfare of children. It is not odd to have doubts regarding the best course to take. Mostly they cannot be resolved quickly and perhaps are best handled by working through step by step.

However, common-sense must recommend that parents should start, even when their child is small, to learn what facilities for respite care are available particularly in the immediate locality, and this will include holiday periods and long-term care.

Local authority and privately-run establishments exist in most areas, though regrettably placements for the severely handicapped are the hardest to find (the parents of these people are most in need of rest periods). Get to know the different kinds of care offered and the philosophy behind their approach. Arrange visits and see for yourself, don't accept others' opinions. Organisations like Camphill Communities welcome visits and the more a parent sees helps a judgment of what is best for the child.

Letting go of a youngster with a handicap is painful for all concerned. Other members of the family, including Grandparents may be upset too. Hopefully, a new environment and daily occupation will offer friends, entertainment and other, as yet unexplored dimensions to their life, but they may take time to settle. The parental heartache can be helped if this move is seen as a positive, next step in 'growing-up'.

It is important too, that parents don't just drift along without taking advice on coping with an adult (over 19) and making sure they understand the necessary processes in providing for their child after they are unable to do so. Thinking of these things naturally causes unease but they must be tackled. Ask questions if possible of parents with offspring older than yours to see how they do things and add constantly to your general knowledge of what is happening to people with a mental handicap. There are considerable changes currently occurring in the way society sees the future for this group of people. It is policy to close large subnormality hospitals and open small homes under the umbrella of 'community care'. This is new and seemingly meeting opposition in some quarters. Nobody can be made to feel compassion and somehow the community at large is frightened of 'the mentally handicapped'. Parents will undoubtedly become aware of these trends and feel helpless in the face of conflicting 'authoritarian' views, but one thing they should not forget is that far from dumping unwanted people on an unwilling community these small homes often generate jobs and may even regenerate the now sadly absent idea that we all must help in some way to care for those who need assistance.

So community care is a challenge to society but should greatly enhance the lives of people with a handicap. However, some will always be too handicapped to fit into this type of care so there will always be a need for communities where a great deal of help is offered. This writer believes that all concerned and informed parents should take all opportunities to inform local authorities of what *parents* believe to be the best life-styles for their sons and daughters.

## The Dilemma

*What's going to happen to her eventually?*
*Who will look after her when you can't?*
*What happens if you die?*
*How long will she live?*
*Questions which seem to obsess people*
*For they have asked since she was small.*

*Of course these things have disturbed my sleep*
*And kept me awake at night.*

*All children must eventually leave their parents*
*In the normal course of things.*

*But she is so very handicapped.*
*And so*
*At the moment*
*It is impossible to find a residential home.*
*In any case we are not ready for the parting yet*
*And nor is she.*
*There is still much progress to make*
*Learning to work through.*

*Then it must be the right place for her -*
*Christ's Christian, loving, calm and wanting to welcome her as*
    *A complete person.*
*Even though she is imperfect to many eyes*
*She is, we know,*
*Perfect in the love she offers*
    *the laughter and joy she radiates*
    *the peace she inspires*
    *the joyous sense of purpose she induces in us.*

*We live in faith that what is right*
*will emerge*
*with the ebb and flow*
    *of time.*

# Glossary

These are just a few terms that may crop up when talking to doctors, physio-therapists, etc. For more specialized terms and medical "labels" it is best to ask the person using the word or to look it up in a medical dictionary or text book.

*Abduction:* Movement of the limbs away from the midline of the body.

*Accommodation:* Ability of the eye to focus at different distances.

*Acuity:* Clarity or sharpness of vision.

*Adduction:* Movement of the limbs towards the midline of the body.

*Aphasia:* Loss of speech, as result of cerebral affection.

*Asymmetrical:* One side of the body different from the other – unequal.

*Ataxic:* A type of cerebral palsy in which the child has no balance; he is jerky and unsteady.

*Athetoid:* A type of cerebral palsy in which the child has uncontrolled and continuously unwanted movements.

*Atrophy:* Wasting of muscles or nerve cells.

*Autism:* Is a difficult condition to put across in words. It includes:
    Difficulty with social relationships.
    Difficulty with verbal communication and non-verbal communication.

Difficulty in the development of play and imagination.

Resistance to change in routine.

An autistic youngster will often display indifference, does not play with other children, has bizarre behaviour, giggles or laughs inappropriately, is echolalic (repeats words endlessly) lacks creative play, etc.

*Automatic movements:* Necessary movements done without thought or effort.

*Binocular Vision:* Ability to use both eyes simultaneously to focus on the same object, fusing the two images into one perception.

*Blindness:* Inability to see; absence or severe reduction of vision.

*Cataract:* Condition in which the crystalline lens of the eye loses transparency, either partially or totally, resulting in the loss of visual acuity.

*Cerebral Palsy:* Disorder of posture and movement resulting from brain damage.

*Cognitive Skills:* Abilities in processing of intellectual material.

*Congenital:* Present at birth or shortly afterwards.

*Contracture:* Permanently tight muscles and joints.

*Cornea:* Transparent portion of the outer coat of the eyeball, forming the front of the aqueous chamber and serving as the eye's major refracting medium.

*Cortical Visual Impairment:* Usually profound visual loss, intact capillary reflexes and normal-appearing eyes following brain damage after an acute respiratory or cardiac arrest.

*Cyanosis:* Blue discolouration due to circulation of imperfectly oxygenated blood.

*Deformities:* Body or limbs fixed in abnormal positions.

*Development:* Growth of the brain and body.

*Developmental Dysphasia:* Delayed development of normal language and speech due to neurological damage.

*Diplegia:* A type of cerebral palsy, the legs being mostly affected.

*Diplopia:* Seeing one object as if it were two.

*Distractable:* Unable to concentrate.

*Down's Syndrome:* A syndrome is a set of symptoms occurring together. Down's Syndrome used to be known as Mongolism. Features include "mongoloid" features, short phalanges, widened space between first and second toes and fingers and a range of mental retardation. Associated with a chromosomal abnormality, usually of chromosome 21.

*Dyslexia:* Impaired ability to read

*Equilibrium:* State of balance.

*Extension:* Straightening of any part of the body.

*Facilitation:* Making it possible to move.

*Field of Vision:* The space within which an object can be seen while the eye remains fixed upon one (central) point, including the limits of peripheral or indirect vision.

*Flexion:* Bending of any part of the body.

*Flaccid:* Floppy. (See Hypotonia).

*Floppy:* Loose or poor posture or movements.

*Functional Vision:* Presence of enough usable vision so that the person has the ability to use sight as a primary channel for learning or living.

*Functionally Blind:* Person whose primary channels for learning and receiving information are tactile and auditory.

*Glaucoma:* Disease of the eye marked by an increase in intraocular pressure causing organic changes in the optic nerve and defects in the visual field.

*Glioma:* Malignant tumour of the retina.

*Head Control:* Ability to control the position of the head.

*Hemiplegia:* A type of cerebral palsy in which only one half of the body is involved.

*Hydrocephalus:* Congenital or acquired condition marked by dilatation of the cerebral ventricles, usually occurring secondarily to obstruction of the cerebro-spinal fluid within the skull. Typically there is enlargement of the head, prominence of the forehead, brain atrophy, mental deterioration and convulsions.

*Hypotonia:* Decreased muscle tension, preventing maintenance of posture against gravity, also difficulty in starting movement due to lack of fixation.

*Motor Skills:* Ability of movement.

*Muscle tone:* The state of tension in muscles at rest and when we move – regulated under normal circumstances sub-consciously in such a way that the tension is sufficiently high to withstand the pull of gravity i.e. to keep us upright, but it is never too strong to interfere with our movements.

*Muscular Dystrophy:* A group of genetically-determined, painless, degenerative myopathies marked by muscular weakness and atrophy without nervous system involvement.

*Myopia:* Near sightedness.

*Neurologist:* A specialist in neurology, the branch of medicine concerned with the nervous system, both normal and in disease.

*Nystagmus:* Continual oscillation (darting movement) of the eyeballs.

*Ocular:* Pertaining to the eye.

*Occupational Therapy:* Treatment given to help the child towards the greatest possible independence in daily living.

*Ophthalmologist:* Doctor of medicine or M.D. who specializes in diagnosis and treatment of defects and diseases of the eye, performing surgery when necessary or prescribing other types of treatment, including eyeglasses or other optical devices.

*Optic Atrophy:* Degeneration of the nerve tissue that carries messages from the retina to the brain.

*Optician:* One who grinds lenses, fits them into frames, dispenses and adjusts glasses or other optical devices on the written prescription of an optometrist or physician.

*Optometrist:* A person qualified to carry out sight testing, including checking the motor co-ordination of the eyes and, where indicated, to prescribe spectacles or contact lenses to correct refractive errors and those anomalies of binocular function which are amenable to optical correction.

*Orthopaedic:* Concerning the branch of surgery dealing with the preservation and restoration of the function of the skeletal system, its articulation and associated structures.

*Orthoptist:* Non-medical technical person who provides scientifically planned exercises for the eye, developing or restoring the normal teamwork of the system.

*Paediatrician:* Specialist in the branch of medicine concerning children.

*Passive:* That which is done to the child without his help or co-operation.

*Pathological:* Abnormal.

*Perception:* The process of organising and interpreting the sensations an individual receives from internal and external stimuli.

*Peripheral Vision:* Perception of objects, motion or colour by any part of the retina, excluding the macula.

*Perseveration:* Unnecessary repetition of movement and/or speech.

*Phonation:* Ability to utter vocal sounds.

*Physiotherapy:* The treatment of disorders of movement.

*Posture:* Position from which the child starts a movement.

*Prader-Willi syndrome:* Was first described in 1956, still an uncommon birth defect (and there are even more uncommon syndromes than Prader-Willi coming to light). Investigations are offering help about its physical and behavioural aspects but as yet the basic cause is undiscovered, thought to be damage to the hypothalamus or mid-brain area development. Abnormalities include small stature and small hands and feet, mental deficiency – I.Q. 20 to 80, commonly 40 to 60, severe back problems like scoliosis or lordosis, obesity and eventually often sugar diabetes.

*Prone:* Lying on tummy.

*Quadriplegia:* A type of cerebral palsy in which the whole body is affected.

*Reflexes:* Postures and movements completely beyond the child's control.

*Retardation:* Slowing down of physical and mental development.

*Retina:* Innermost coating of the eye, containing light-sensitive nerve cells and fibres connecting with the brain via the optic nerve.

*Righting:* Ability to put head and body right when positions are abnormal or uncomfortable.

*Rigidity:* Very stiff posture and movements.

*Rotation:* Movement that takes place between hip and shoulder or vice versa.

*Spasm:* Sudden tightening of muscles.

*Spasticity:* Stiffness.

*Spatial:* Relationship of one thing to another in space learned through vision and movement.

*Speech Therapy:* Treatment given to develop and to improve speech and to help with feeding problems.

*Squint:* One eye only looks at the object whilst the other deviates. The latter can be inwards (convergent), outwards (divergent) or upwards or downwards (vertical).

*Stimulation:* Provide the desire to move, speak, etc.

*Supine:* Lying on back.

*Symmetrical:* Both sides equal.

*Syndrome:* A set of of symptoms occurring together e.g. Down's Syndrome.

*Tonic neck reflex:* When the turning of the head causes one arm to straighten and stiffen and the other to bend and stiffen.

*Voluntary movements:* Movements done with intention and with concentration.

# Recommended Reading

Althea, *I use a Wheelchair*, Dinosaur Publications, 1983, London. A picture book for children with carefully and sensitively worded text – for the wheelchair user, or for siblings and friends.

Althea, *Special Care Babies*, Dinosaur Publications, 1986, London. Written and illustrated for young children, explaining in a reassuring way about tiny babies in special units, what is done for them and why. Ideal for siblings during or after the event.

Bowlby, John, *Child Care and the Growth of Love*, Penguin-Pelican Books, 1953. Good on general child development.

Brewster, Dorothy, *You can Breastfeed Your Baby... Even in Special Situations*, Rodale Press, Emmaus, Pa, 1979.

Cotton, Esther, *Conductive Education and Cerebral Palsy*, The Spastics Society, 1981. The essentials of conductive education as developed in Budapest. Leaflet available from:
The Spastics Society, 12 Park Crescent, London WIN 4EQ.

Farino, S. and O'Reilly, A., *Hawaii Early Learning Profile (HELP)* Vort Co., P.O. 11132 Pao Alto, Ca 94306, 1979. Excellent guide to suggested activities in all developmental areas.

Featherstone, Helen, *A Difference in the Family*, Harper and Row, New York, 1980.

Finnie, Nancie R., *Handling the Young Cerebral Palsied Child at Home*, Heinemann Medical Books Ltd., London, 1984. An invaluable book that seems to be used by many professionals one comes into contact with.

Freeman, Peggy, *Understanding the Deaf/Blind Child,* Heinemann Health Books, London, 1975. Superb book – helpful for no hearing loss or any combination of impairment. Helpful from birth onwards.

Freeman, Peggy. *The Deaf/Blind Baby,* Heinemann Medical Books Ltd. London, 1985. A programme of care.

Greenfield, Josh. The Noah Series: *A Child called Noah* (1972), *A Place for Noah* (1978) and *A Client called Noah* (1986) all by Henry Holt and Co. New York.

Haslam, Dr David, *Sleepless Children*, Judy Piatkus Publishers, Ltd., 1984.

Levy, Janine. *The Baby Exercise Book,* (Translated from the French), Pantheon Books, New York, 1973.

Lloyd, Janette, *Jacob's Ladder: A Parent's View of Portage,* Costello Educational Press, Tunbridge Wells, 1986. The story of "pioneering" Portage, used with a child with Down's Syndrome

Montagu, Ashley, *Touching: The Human Significance of the Skin,* Columbia University Press, 1971.

Nolan, Christopher, *Under the Eye of the Clock,* Pan Paperback, 1988. Prize winning autobiography of C. Nolan, who nearly died at birth but survived with no limb control.

Perske, Robert and Martha, *Hope for the Families,* Abingdon Press, Nashville, Tennessee, 1981. Important for its view of social attitudes.

Sanctuary, Gerald, *After I'm Gone, What Will Happen to My Handicapped Child?* Souvenir Press, 1985. Practical advice on providing for the future, including sound legal information.

Warner, Jennifer, *Helping the Handicapped Child with Early Feeding*, Winslow Press, 1981.

Williams, P. and Schoultz B., *We Can Speak for Ourselves*, Indiana University Press, 1984. Self-advocacy for mentally handicapped people.

Wing, Lorna, *Autistic Children: A Guide for Parents*, Constable, 1980.

Winnicott, D. W., *The Child, The Family and the Outside World*, Penguin, 1984.

# Useful Addresses: U.K.

Association for Spina Bifida and Hydrocephalus,
22 Upper Woburn Place, London WC1H 0EP. Telephone: 01-388 1382.
(Publish excellent magazine, *Link*.)

Birmingham Institute for Conductive Education,
Bell Hill, Northfield, Birmingham B31 1LD.

British Epilepsy Association, Ansley House, 40 Hanover Square, Leeds LS3 1BE.

Cleft Lip and Palate Association, Mrs Cy Thirlaway,
1 Eastwood Gardens, Kenton, Newcastle-upon-Tyne NE3 3DQ.

Conductive Education Association,
c/o Mrs M. Lily, B.A.O.T., 7 West End Avenue, Pinner, Middlesex HA5 1BH.

Cystic Fibrosis Research Trust,
Alexandra House, 5 Blyth Road, Bromley, Kent BR1 3RS.

Down's Childrens' Association,
12/13 Clapham Common, Southside, London SW4 7AA.
Telephone: 01-720 0008. (Produces an excellent notebook: *You've had a Down's Syndrome Baby? Perhaps We Can Help?*)

Gingerbread (Single Parents), 35 Wellington Street, London WC2E 7BN.

Heartline (for children with heart defects),
5 Russet Gardens, Camberley, Surrey.

La Leche League, BM 3424, London WC1N 3XX. 24-hour Telephone 01-242 1278
Also: P.O. Box 1280, Raheny, Dublin 5, Eire.

MENCAP (Royal Society for Mentally Handicapped Children and Adults),
117-123 Golden Lane, London EC1Y ORF.

Multiple Sclerosis Society, 25 Effie Road, London SW6 1EE.

Muscular Dystrophy Group,
Nattrass House, 35 Macaulay Road, London SW4 0QP.

National Association for Welfare of Children in Hospital,
Argyl House, 29-31 Euston Road, London NW1 2SD.

National Autistic Society, 276 Willesden Lane, London NW2 5RB.

National Childbirth Trust, 9 Queensborough Terrace, London W2 3TB.

National Portage Project Association,
King Alfred's College, Sparkford Road, Winchester, Hampshire.

Royal National Institute for the Blind,
224 Great Portland Street, London W1N 6AA.

Royal National Institute for the Deaf, 105 Gower Street, London WC1E 6AH.

SENSE (National Association for Deaf-Blind),
311 Grays Inn Road, London WC1X 8PT.

Share-A-Care (National Register for Rare Diseases will link people with similar
diseases), 8 Cornmarket, Faringdon, Oxon.

The Spastics Society, 12 Park Crescent, London W1N 4EQ. And the Society's
College: Castle Priory College, Thames Street, Wallingford, Oxon. OX10 OHE.
Telephone (0491) 37551. (The college conducts useful seminars and courses on
all aspects of disability – open to parents and professionals.)

# Useful Addresses: U.S.A.

American Foundation for the Blind,
15 West Sixteenth Street, New York, N.Y. 10011.

Cleft Parent Guild (Cleft Palate),
c/o Crippled Children's Society, 7120 Franklin Ave., Los Angeles, C.A. 90046.

Closer Look (Guide to services in different States),
Box 1492, Washington, D.C. 20013.

Cystic Fibrosis Foundation, 3379 Peachtree Road, N.E., Atlanta GA 30326.

Epilepsy Foundation of America,
1828 L Street, N.W., Suite 406, Washington, D.C. 20036.

La Leche League, 9616 Minneapolis Ave., Franklin Park, Ill. 60131.
Telephone: (312) 455 7730.

Muscular Dystrophy Association, Inc.,
810 Seventh Ave., New York, N.Y. 10019.

National Association of the Deaf, 814 Thayer Avenue, Silver Spring, MD 20910.

National Association for Down's Syndrome, P.O. Box 63, Oak Park, Ill. 60303.

National Center for Education in Maternal and Child Health,
38th and R Street, N.W., Washington D.C. 20057. Telephone: (202) 625 8400
(For National lists of voluntary organisations.)

National Institute of Child and Human Development, 9000 Rockville Pike, Bethesda, Md. 20892. Telephone: (301) 496 5133 (For information specialist.)

National Mental Health Association,
1021 Prince Street, Alexandria, Va. 22314-2971.

National Society for Autistic Children, 169 Tampa Ave., Albany N.Y. 12208.

Parents without Partners,
7910 Woodmont Ave., Suite 1000, Washington D.C. 20014.

Portage Project, Cesa 12, Box 564, Portage, Wisconsin 53901.

Spina Bifida Association, 343 South Dearborn, Chicago, Ill. 60604.

United Cerebral Palsy Association,
122 East 23rd Street, New York, N.Y. 10010.

# Notes

## U.K.

Toys for the Handicapped, 76 Barracks Road, Sandy Lane Industrial Estate, Stourport on Severn, Worcs. DY13 9QB. Telephone: (0299) 827820 (Free catalogue on request.)

National Library for the Handicapped Child, University of London Institute of Education, 20 Bedford Way, London WC1H 0AL.
Telephone: 01-636 1500 ext. 599 (After hours: 01-255 1363).

*Orange Badge Scheme for the Disabled:* If your child is visually-handicapped or has other handicaps affecting mobility, he may be entitled to concessions and special treatment regarding the use of the car and parking – the Orange Badge Scheme. Your G.P. will initiate registration.

## U.S.A.

*The Exceptional Parent* is a helpful and informative magazine published eight times a year for parents, carers, teachers and disabled adults. Available from: The Exceptional Parent, 605 Commonwealth Avenue, Boston, MA 02215.

For indoor and outdoor toys suitable for children with handicaps:
English Garden Toys Ltd., P.O. Box 786, Indianola, Pa 15051.
Telephone: (412) 767 5332.

# Authors

Moyna E. (Paddy) Clarke in her life before Sam, was a teacher, college lecturer, journalist and trained in business management.

Since Sam's arrival she has continued to write and lecture (in food sciences and English) taken a qualification teaching those with learning problems and acquired a B.A. (Hons) degree. She has also been Managing Director of a food company run in conjunction with her husband. Currently she lectures in creative writing and literature and has embarked on a M.A. in Special Education.

Holly Kofsky is currently an active participant in San Francisco's Support for Parents of Special Children organization, and is training as a representative of their outreach programme which helps parents come to terms with their children's special needs. She attended a Waldorf School for eleven years as a child, and graduated from the Spring Valley School of Eurythmy in 1980. Holly's work with her own two special children has led her to interests in a wide range of Therapeutic methodologies.

A native of California, Jennifer (Burtt) Lauruol earned a B.A. in Modern Languages from the University of California, Santa Barbara, and studied in Germany and England. She and her French husband, Jacques, lived for seven years in Strasbourg, France where their children were born, and where Jennifer worked as a primary school teacher, language tutor and freelance translator. In 1986 the Lauruols settled in Gloucester, England.

Helen Allen did a degree in history and politics and met her partner Trevor while at University. She has worked as a vegetarian cook and began training to become a homeopath. She hopes to continue this and practice professionally when her children are older. At present she is actively immersed in motherhood.

Lyndsey Gill worked as a medical secretary for General Practitioners, a Consultant Radiotherapist and a Consultant Paediatrician before having her family. She is the mother of Laurie, aged 3½ years who has cerebral palsy and is quadriplegic and visually handicapped, and of Jesse, aged 1½ years. Lyndsey compiled *To A Different Drumbeat's* glossary, basing it on working knowledge of medical terms and meanings.

**LIFEWAYS. Working with family questions.**
Gudrun Davy and Bons Voors.

*Lifeways* is about children, about family life, about being a parent. But most of all it is about freedom, and how the tension between family life and personal fulfillment can be resolved.

*'These essays affirm that creating a family, even if you are a father on your own, or a working mother, can be a joyful, positive and spiritual work. The first essay is one of the wisest and balanced discussions of women's rôles I have read.'*

Fiona Handley, Church of England Newspaper.

Paperback; colour cover; 150mm × 210mm; 316pp. ISBN 0 950 706 24 8.
Third impression 1985. Lifeways is published in German and Dutch.

**FESTIVALS, FAMILY AND FOOD**
Diana Carey and Judy Large.

This is a resource book for exploring the festivals – those 'feast days' scattered round the year which children love celebrating. It was written in response to children and busy parents asking, 'What can we do at Christmas and Easter? What games can we play? What can we make?'

*An invaluable resource book.* The Observer

200mm × 225mm; limp bound; 216pp; colour cover; several hundred illustrations. ISBN 0 950 706 23 X.

**THE CHILDREN'S YEAR**
**Crafts and clothes for children to make.**
Stephanie Cooper, Christine Fynes-Clinton and Marye Rowling.

Here is a book which hopes to give the possibility to adults and children alike to rediscover the joy and satisfaction of making something that they know looks and feels good and which can also be played with imaginatively. It takes us through Spring, Summer, Autumn and Winter with appropriate gifts and toys to create, including full, clear instructions and illustrations. There is children's clothing as well, particularly meant to be made of natural fabrics to let the child's body breathe while growing. There are soft items for play and beauty, and there are firm solid wooden ones; moving toys such as balancing birds or climbing gnomes; horses which move when you add children to them! From woolly hats to play houses, mobiles or dolls, here are 112 potential treasures to make in seasonal groupings.

You needn't be an experienced crafts person to create something lovely, and the illustrations make it a joy to browse through while choosing what to make first. *The Children's Year* offers handwork for all ages and individualities, it reminds us of the process of creating as opposed to merely consuming, and all this in the context of nature's rhythm through the year.

The authors are parents who have tried and tested the things to make included in *The Children's Year* with their own families.

Paperback; full colour cover; 267mm × 216mm; 220pp; several hundred illustrations.
ISBN 1 869 890 00 0


## THE INCARNATING CHILD
Joan Salter

Even in today's modern technological world the mystery and miracle of conception, pregnancy and birth stir within many people as a sense of wonder. *The Incarnating child* picks up Wordsworth's theme – "our birth is but a sleep and a forgetting...", and follows the Soul life of tiny babies well into childhood. It is full of practical advice for mothers, fathers, relations or anyone concerned with childcare. Joan Salter examines pregnancy, birth, early infancy, babyhood, childhood, on up to adolescence. She addresses physical and spiritual development, the formation of healthy personalities, nutrition, clothing, environment, toys and learning, immunization and health, and the acquisition of skills and thinking ability. She writes with an astounding attention to detail, and the voice of years of experience in her field.

Joan Salter is a specialist in maternal and childcare, and has a nursing background which included work with migrants from many countries. She is the founder and a director of the Gabriel Baby Centre, since 1976 a centre for maternal and child welfare in Melbourne, and is essentially concerned with the upbringing of the child in the home.

Family and children; colour cover; 210mm × 135mm; sewn limp bound; 224pp; illustrations and photos; ISBN 1 869 890 04 3.


## BETWEEN FORM AND FREEDOM
**A practical guide to the teenage years.**
Betty Staley

*Between Form and Freedom* offers a wealth of insights about teenagers. There are sections on the nature of adolescence – the search for the self, the birth of intellect, the release of feeling, male-female differences and character. Teenagers' needs are explored in relation to family, friends, schools, the arts and love. Issues such as stress, depression, drugs, alcohol and eating disorders are included.

Betty Staley has taught literature with teenagers for many years. She teaches at the Sacramento Waldorf School, runs workshops, serves on the Rudolf Steiner College faculty and wrote for *Ariadne's Awakening*. Her three children are now grown up.

Reviewed in *Mothering* Autumn 1988

*In this excellent book, Betty Staley has given us a compassionate, intelligent, and intuitive look into the minds of children and adolescents. Even the most casual reader of this book will never again respond to children and adolescents in the old mechanical ways... Naively, one could wish this work were a best seller. Practically, I can only hope it will be read by a significant number of significant people _ namely, parents, teachers, and, indeed, adolescents themselves.*
                                                    Joseph Chilton Pearce, author of *The Magical Child*.

210mm × 135mm; sewn limpbound; 320pp; 5 illustrations; colour cover; ISBN 1 869 890 08 6

## ARIADNE'S AWAKENING
**Taking up the threads of consciousness**
Signe Schaefer, Betty Staley and Margli Matthews

Much has been written about women and men in terms of role, gender, and social forms through the ages. The past two decades have witnessed widespread changes in 'rights' and quality on external levels, but this has not always made for more human fulfillment. The authors acknowledge the broad contest of feminism, but broaden its picture enormously. They view 'masculine' and 'feminine' not just as bodily forms, but as principle of meaning: principles at work within each of us, in society and indeed in the entire span of evolution.

*Ariadne's Awakening* traces through myth and history the growing human kind has made up to the present; it considers, phases of life, relationships for men and women, and confronts such issues as the scientific management of conception and death, the rape of Earth, 'natural resources and the need for a New Feminine to influence values and decisions for the future.

Paperback; 210mm × 135mm; 224pp ISBN 1 869 890 01 9

## *Orders*

If you have difficulties ordering from a bookshop, you can order direct from Hawthorn Press, Bankfield House, 13 Wallbridge, Stroud GL5 3JA. Telephone (045 36) 77040 Fax (045 36) 73295